JEWELRY MAKING

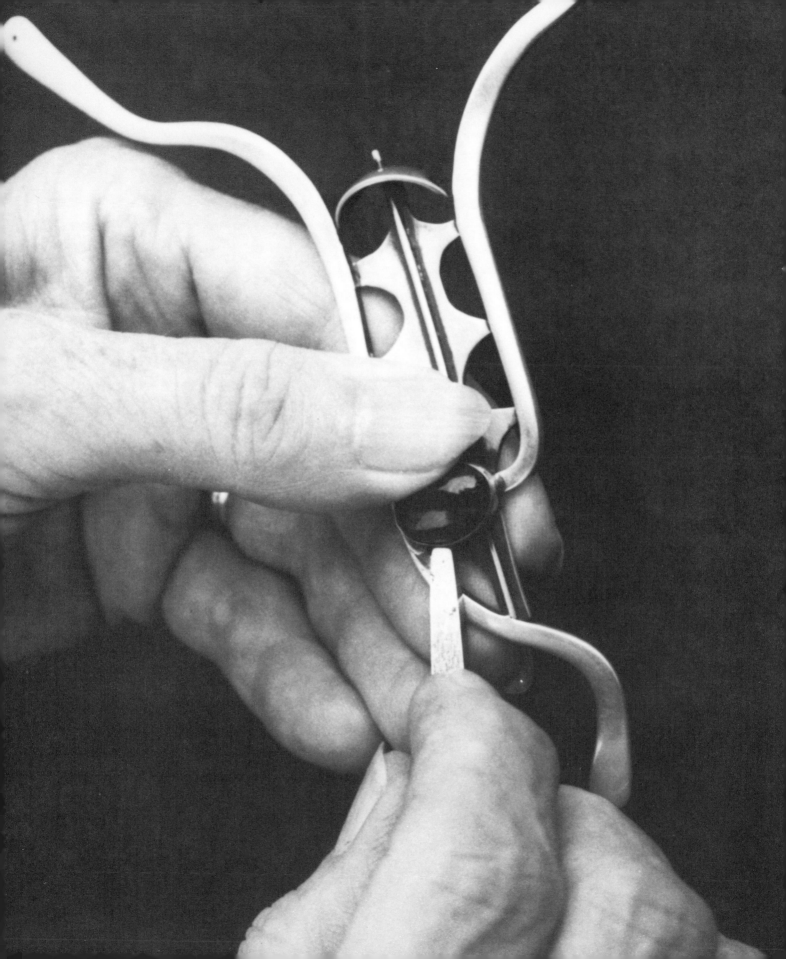

JEWELRY MAKING
A Guide for Beginners

Theodore P. Foote

Davis Publications, Inc.
Worcester, Massachusetts

left: Setting the edge of a bezel with a stone pusher. A small section at a time is pushed into place from alternating opposite sides of the stone.

ACKNOWLEDGMENTS

Grateful acknowledgment is given for the assistance of the following people in developing this book: to my wife, Coletta, for her encouragement, numerous hours of typing and other secretarial work; to George F. Horn for encouragement and advice; to Mary M. Calemine for her review of the manuscript; to Mary M. Hosken for her typing assistance.

I appreciate the cooperation of the librarians of the American Craft Council; The Metropolitan Museum of Art, Department of Prints and Photographic Services; The American Museum of Natural History, Photographic Collection Library.

Finally, a special expression of gratitude is given to the following craftspersons who graciously shared their time and energies to provide photographs of their creative work:

Carol Anspach, Marilyn Davidson, Arline M. Fisch, John T. Fix, Clifford H. Herrold, Mary Lee Hu, Deborah E. Love Jemmott, David W. Keens, Marcia Lewis, Charles Loloma, Bob Natalini, and Clara Schlegel.

Front Cover: Symmetrical rhythmic line movements interact to emphasize the central form in this pendant designed by the author. Sterling silver, forged and constructed with lapis lazuli. Collection of Mrs. Susan M. Kolb.

Back Cover: Hand pendant by Bob Natalini. This picture captures the iridescence of the beetle parts under the Plexiglas window.

To Sue and Phil

Printed in the United States of America
Library of Congress Catalog Card Number: 80-67547
ISBN: 0-87192-130-8

Composition: Davis Press, Inc.
Type: Sabon
Graphic Design: Jean Hodge

10   9   8   7   6   5   4   3   2   1

Contents

Introduction

above: Necklace, gold and silver, Etruscan, sixth century B.C. The Metropolitan Museum of Art, New York, Rogers Fund, 1913.

left: The Quimbaya people who inhabited the northwestern part of present-day Colombia were among the most skillful goldsmiths of the New World (c. 1300–1500). This collection includes chisels, figurines, nose ornaments, tweezers, a chestplate, and pendants. The chestplate in the bottom center is an abstraction of the human figure. Courtesy of the American Museum of Natural History, New York.

People have adorned themselves with jewelry throughout history. Long before metals were discovered, early humans decorated their bodies with jewelry crafted from basic materials. They used shells to create pendants, made strings of beads from the teeth and claws of animals, and fashioned animal bone into body ornaments.

The discovery of bronze and later, iron, led to the development of tools that were strong and durable extensions of the human hand, allowing ancient craftspeople to create more intricate and personal, often mystical, forms of body adornment.

As civilization progressed from a tribal level, in which tribe members produced only for their own use, to a community level, in which they produced for others, the jewelry maker was one of the many artisans who filled a need in the larger community.

One of the earliest records of jewelry making was left by the Egyptians. A wall painting in the Tomb of the Two Sculptors in ancient Thebes (site of the present-day Luxor and Karnak) depicts the varied activities of an ancient Egyptian jewelry shop. Fortunately, samples of the ancient Egyptians' fine jewelry were preserved, having been buried with the mummified bodies of their rulers and in the graves of their dead. The magical powers believed to reside in these figures and symbols were thought to protect the deceased as they journeyed to the final kingdom. A mystique was also attached to gemstones. Agate was believed to provide protection against spiders and thunderstorms; green jasper was supposed to bring rain; and lapis lazuli was thought by the Egyptians to ward off snakes.

Although Egyptian jewelers created a wide variety of body adornments, beads were the universal jewelry in Egypt. They graced the appearance of rulers, warriors, and workers alike. Beads of gemstone, glass, and clay were etched with symbols believed to protect the wearer from danger.

The long history of jewelry making that began with the Egyptians is a varied and rich heritage that can serve today's jewelry maker as a sensitizing, inspirational resource.

After the decline of Egyptian civilization, power and cultural dominance shifted to the Phoenicians and Greeks. They built upon the design and constuction techniques they had learned from the Egyptians to create jewelry for flourishing new cultures.

The Etruscans developed an advanced and prosperous civilization in western Italy long before Rome's rise to greatness. As seafarers, they were exposed to the cultural richness of Greece and the Orient, which influenced their use of materials and tools in their jewelry and other art forms.

The Romans' early art was adapted from the nations they conquered. Their jewelry making skills and designs reflected the influences of many peoples and eventually spread throughout the Roman empire. With the fall of Rome and the intermingling of peoples during the many wars that followed, the art forms that emerged were influenced by cultures of the Orient and the Middle East as well as Europe.

Religion played a part in a resurgence of art. During the Middle Ages, the spread of Christianity created a demand for the work of artists and artisans to decorate churches and cathedrals. Many guilds of goldsmiths and gem cutters that came into being in the early Middle Ages were

Artisans and apprentices in an Egyptian jewelry shop work under the direction of a master craftsman in this wall scene painted around 1500 B.C. It is located in the Tomb of the Two Sculptors in Thebes. The Metropolitan Museum of Art, New York.

Primitive pectoral from Oceanic-Melanasia. Solomon Islands, Santa Cruz Island. Made from Tridacna shell, turtle shell, and cord. 7⅜-inches (18.7 cm) wide. The Metropolitan Museum of Art, New York, The Michael C. Rockefeller Memorial Collection of Primitive Art, 1958.

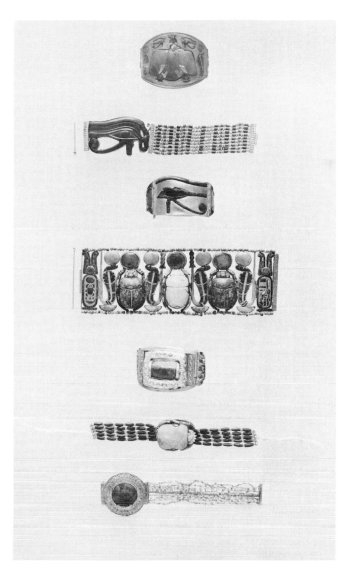

Bracelets from the Tomb of Tutankhamen. A variety of gems were used in these symbols that held special meaning for the Egyptians. Photography by the Egyptian Expedition. The Metropolitan Museum of Art, New York.

Gold bracelets set with pearls and sapphires. Byzantine, probably sixth century A.D. The Metropolitan Museum of Art, New York, gift of J. Pierpont Morgan, 1917.

The intricate inlays and beadwork on this pectoral from the Tomb of Tutankhamen demonstrate superb lapidary and construction skills. Photography by the Egyptian Expedition. The Metropolitan Museum of Art, New York.

semireligious organizations. One of the prime purposes of the guilds was to protect and maintain standards of quality. The apprentice to journeyman to master-craftsman system of proficiency developed in the guilds and was strictly followed and enforced. The education of a goldsmith-jeweler was a long, thorough, and detailed process. Like the ancient Egyptian counterpart, the medieval jeweler became expert in every aspect of the craft.

The culture of the Western World exploded during the Renaissance. Suddenly, the entire range of the arts soared to new heights of intellectual and artistic achievement and the ever increasing demand for their creations spurred artists and craftspeople to create even greater masterpieces. Almost overnight, arts and crafts displayed an ornateness in every design theme.

Many superb painters and sculptors of this period began their careers as apprentice goldsmiths. Sandro Botticelli, Lorenzo Ghiberti, Luca della Robbia, Baccio Baudinnelli, Andrea del Sarto, and Albrecht Dürer all served such apprenticeships. Hans Holbein designed some of the jewelry worn by Henry VIII, an ardent jewelry collector who delighted in decorating himself. His collection included 324 brooches and 234 rings.

Versatile, flamboyant Benvenuto Cellini resented the practice of having jewelry designed by painters who were not skilled as goldsmiths. However, the practice spread throughout Europe because many of the goldsmiths felt that the beauty of their works was enhanced by the painters' designing skills and by the expertly-drafted patterns they supplied.

One of the major developments in jewelry technology occurred in the late sixteenth century when diamonds were first cut with a metal disc coated with a diamond dust solution. Louis de Berquem of Bruges is credited with the development of this faceting process in which a series of flat surfaces are cut in a planned order on a hemisphere shape and then polished. Lapidaries in India may have inspired de Berquem's process since they had been using a cutting process to remove flaws from gemstones for many years. The artisans trained by de Berquem eventually established their own workshops and later founded the gem cutting centers in Amsterdam and Antwerp.

During the centuries that followed the Renaissance, processes were refined and new sources of precious metals and stones were located. The improvement of machines and manufacturing techniques helped to supply a growing international market for jewelry.

The heritage of jewelry antedates the history of Europe

and the Middle East. The need for adornment and the development of techniques, skills, and forms to satisfy that need occurred in every age and every civilization. The immemorial and universal use of jewelry is revealed in the histories of the tribal societies and kingdoms of Africa and the Pacific; in the dynasties and kingdoms of China, India and Japan; and in the Aztec, Mayan, and Inca cultures of the Americas.

In this century, the advent of inexpensive metals, synthetic jewels, and mass production techniques have made jewelry accessible to everyone, although these factors often compromise its durability and beauty.

Technology has provided exceedingly well for our functional needs, but the standardization of mass production can have a dulling effect on our artistic value system. However, we have seen an increased sensitivity among American consumers within the past twenty years. More and more people want to own something unusual. We have witnessed an unprecedented revival of crafts in the United States. People are seeking the uniqueness that only the skill of talented handcrafters can ensure.

Jewelry has played a vital role in the crafts renaissance. Contemporary jewelry makers have responded with exciting creations for the aesthetic sense and expectations of consumers. Their works have become innovative expressions of their thoughts about design, their beliefs about jewelry as an art form, and their mastery of the skills of the craft.

Pendant, gold, crystal, enamel, pearl, and rubies made by German goldsmiths c. 1600. Metropolitan Museum of Art, New York, The Michael Friedsam Collection, Bequest of Michael Friedsam, 1931.

Chinese hair ornaments in the form of spiders and spider webs made from silver. Ming Dynasty, 1368–1644. The Metropolitan Museum of Art, New York, Fletcher Fund, 1925.

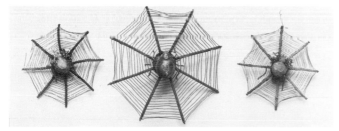

Gold earrings, Greater Sinu area, Colombia. Twelfth to sixteenth centuries. The Metropolitan Museum of Art, New York, gift of Mrs. Harold L. Bache, 1974.

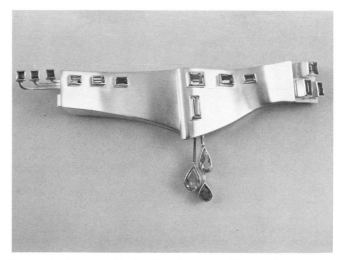

Rectangular brooch by Marilyn Davidson, 1979. Silver, rubies, garnets, andalusites, topaz, tourmalines, citrine, aquamarine, iolite, sapphire. 5" × 2½" (12.7 cm × 6.4 cm).

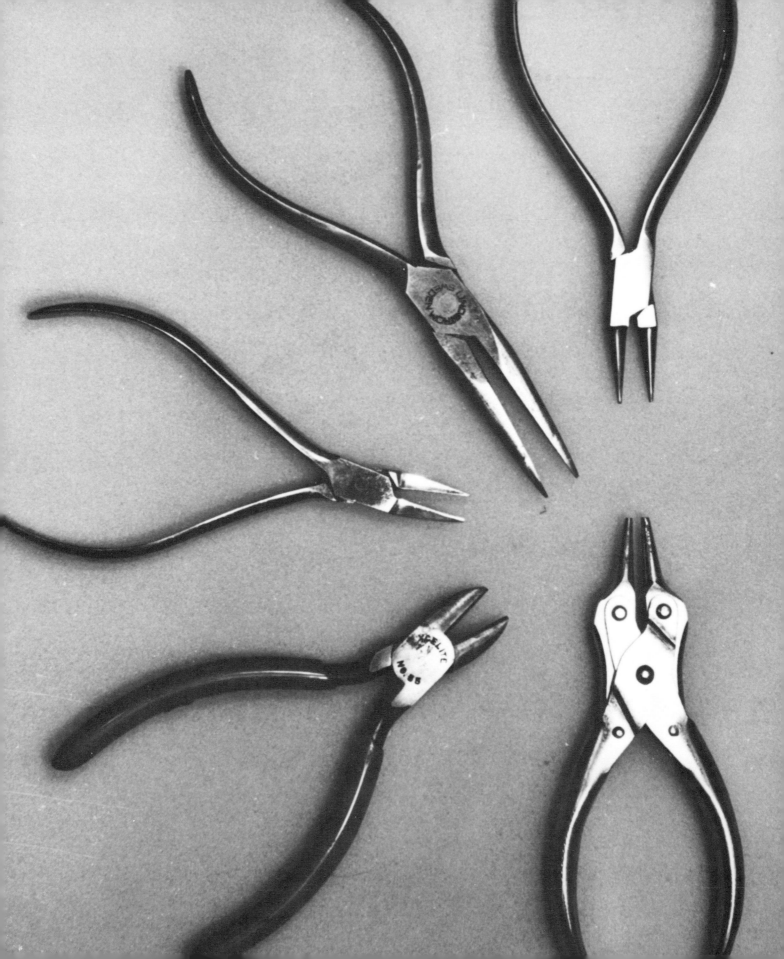

CHAPTER I

Tools, Materials
&
Supplies

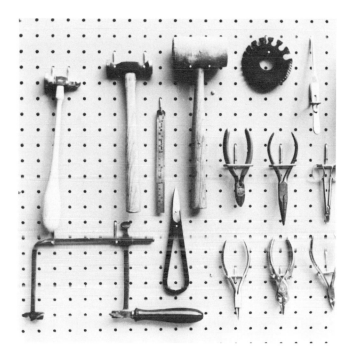

above: A pegboard panel mounted close to the work area can store and organize tools.

left: Some of the pliers used in jewelry making. From left to right: round nose, chain nose, flat nose, diagonal cutters, and parallel jaw round nose.

Literally thousands of tools, ranging from basic instruments for cutting and forming to highly specialized devices intended for a single function in a special technique, are available to the jewelry maker. In this book, only the tools required for the processes described in the text will be listed. As the jewelry maker's skills and design concepts develop, it may be necessary to expand one's tool collection to enhance performance capability.

Tools have been designed for specific jewelry making functions, and an essential rule to follow is to use the correct tool for the operation being performed. A second basic rule is that tools require care. Striking a stamping tool or a punch with a planishing hammer will ruin the face of the hammer because the stamping tools and punches are made from harder steel. Storing files so that they rub each other will dull their cutting edges. Leaving a blade under tension in a saw frame over an extended period of time will reduce the frame's ability to hold the blade taut. Moisture, oils, and dirt can ruin the working surfaces of jewelry tools. Care should be taken to protect them from these hazards. Tools should be wiped with a dry, clean cloth after use or whenever they appear contaminated. Tools that will be stored over a period of time should be thinly coated with light protective oil. A continuing concern for the proper use and care of tools will make a classroom or studio much less costly to operate.

Take the time necessary to develop and maintain an organized storage system for tools. The effectiveness of the tools will be preserved for a longer time and work procedures will be more efficient. A pegboard panel mounted within easy reach of the work area can be used to hang hammers, saws, snips, pliers, and similar tools. Blocks of wood can be drilled to hold needle files, drill bits, punches, and scribers. Compartmented drawers, plastic storage boxes and bins can also be used to develop an effective storage system for other tools and supplies.

Beginning Tools

Jeweler's saw frame holds the cutting blades called piercing saws or jeweler's saw blades. It comes in various throat depths (the vertical distance between the back of the blade and the back of the adjustable bar of the frame), which range from 2¼ inches to 8 inches. A 5-inch saw frame is ideal for most studio work. The frame can be adjusted to use broken blades and to set and maintain proper blade tension.

Blades are sized by number: the finest is 8/o, the coarsest 14. Sizes 4/o, 2/o, and o are used most frequently.

Bench pin clamps to the workbench and supports the object being sawed. The side facing the bench has a smooth anvil surface. When wooden pins are purchased without a cutout, a V-shape must be cut into the bevelled end of the pin with a coping or mitre saw. A bench pin can be made by cutting a V-shaped slot into one end of a 2¼-inch × 6½-inch × ¾-inch piece of wood. The pin can then be attached to the bench with a C-clamp.

Hand drill, pin vise, and drill bits are basic to metal work, especially in pierced work and certain fittings. Drill bits from 1/16-inch to larger sizes work well in the hand drill. Bits smaller than 1/16-inch should be used in a pin vise. Small bits are sized by number (Appendix II lists the decimal equivalent in inches for the number size). A range

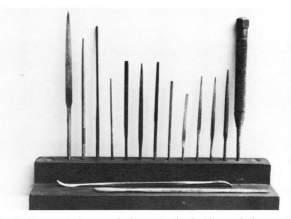

Needle files can be kept ready for use in this holder made from a drilled block of wood.

Jeweler's saw frame and saw blades.

Bench pin.

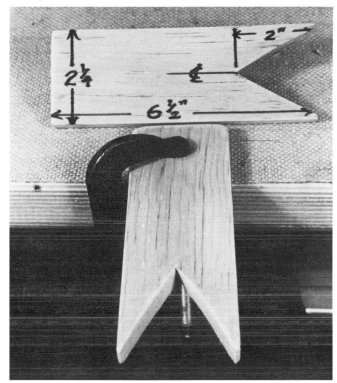

A bench pin cut from wood ¾-inches (1.9 cm) thick and fastened to the workbench with a "C"-clamp.

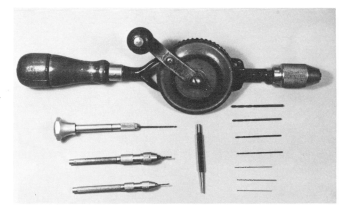

Hand drill, pin vises, drill bits, and a center punch.

Cutting tools. Top to bottom: jeweler's snips, bezel snips, wire nippers, and aviation snips.

of sizes is needed, including some bits that match the guage (thickness) of wire to be used in making jewelry.

Center punch is used to mark the location for drilling. By tapping the punch with a light hammer, a depression is formed which makes a good starting point for drilling. This reduces the possibility of the bit's drifting and marring the surface of the work.

Nippers are wire cutters. The parallel jaw of the common diagonal cutter peaks the wire ends which should be filed flat. Nippers with full-flush edges that make a flat cut across wire are also available. These are designed for cutting thin gauge soft wire. Cutting steel or other hard metal wire will dull the nipper.

Jeweler's snips are used to cut light gauge sheet metal and for cutting solder into small pieces. The seven-inch (17.8 cm) size with a 1½-inch (3.8 cm) cutting blade is ideal for general jewely use.

Tinner's snips are heavy-duty shears used to cut long strips of sheet metal.

Aviation snips are similar to tinner's snips, but have spring loaded handles that reopen the blades and a compound leverage action that exerts more cutting force.

Files are cutting tools, but their primary function in jewelry making is to refine shapes and surfaces. A file selection should include several 6-inch (15.2 cm) pattern

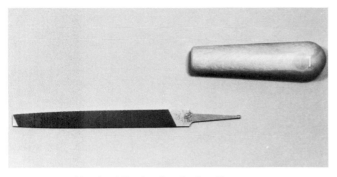

Large pattern files should be fitted with a handle.

Lead block on polished bench block with a planishing hammer.

File card for cleaning files.

Left to right: planishing, silversmith's, peening, and chasing hammers.

files in either barrette, half round, pillar, three square, or round shapes. File cuts range from 2/0 (coarse) to 6 (fine). Cuts 2, 3, and 4 are used most often. Several differently shaped needle files should also be obtained, and they should be a number 4 cut for fine work. Several riffle files for smoothing metal in tight places should also be obtained.

The smooth, pointed flat end of the pattern file, called the *tang*, should be fitted with a secure handle as a safety precaution.

A file card is used to remove bits of metal that clog files. The file card has one face of stiff bristles and another of short steel wires. Files should be cleaned regularly to remove the metal that becomes imbedded between the cutting edges (teeth).

Pliers are a versatile tool used to hold, shape, and manipulate wire and small pieces of metal. Many sizes of jeweler's pliers are made, but the following ones, in a 4½-inch (11.4 cm) to 5-inch (12.7 cm) size, are essential.

Round nose to bend and shape wire.

Chain nose, or snipe nose, to make links and loops.

Flat nose to make angular bends in wire and strips.

The bench block is a highly polished, hardened steel block on which metal is flattened, forged, and stamped.

Care should be exercised to protect the block surface from rust and scratches and from the splashings of water and cleaning solutions. The surface should be wiped with a clean, dry cloth after use. Before storing the block, coat the surface with a light oil to protect it from rust.

The lead block provides a forming surface for doming and cupping sheet metal. The lead gives beneath the metal as it is pounded. Metal shaped on a lead block should be cleaned thoroughly before it is heated or soldered because the smallest unremoved lead particle will cause pitting.

Hammers are indispensable in jewelry making. The following types are frequently used.

Chasing hammers are used for rivet setting and with chasing and stamping tools.

Ball peen hammers are used for shaping and forging metal.

Planishing hammers are used for forming, removing dents, and smoothing metal. One face is flat and smooth, the other is slightly domed.

Mallets made from nylon, rubber, rawhide or leather will not mar or stretch the surface of metal. They are used to shape rings and bracelets around mandrels and also to flatten sheets and strips of metal.

The ring clamp is a double-ended clamping device that locks objects in one end when the other end is spread with a wedge. The leather faces of the clamp prevent marring

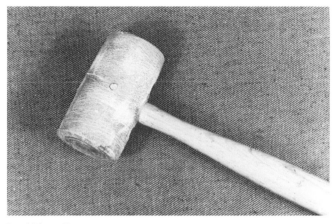

Rawhide mallet.

A table vise with jaws that can lock in many positions is ideally suited for jewelry making.

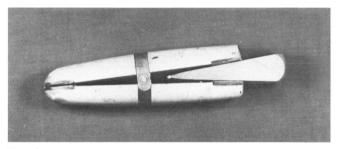

Ring clamp.

or abrading when filing, polishing, and stone setting.

The table vise is ideal for jewelry work. The replaceable jaws are made from nonmarring nylon and the ball and socket arrangement enables you to tilt the article being worked into almost any position.

Mandrels and dapping blocks are forms on which metal is hammered into shape. The *ring mandrel* is a tapered, polished, and hardened steel rod calibrated in ring sizes which is used to shape or enlarge rings and bands of metal. A *bracelet mandrel* is used to forge and shape bracelets and is available in round or oval shape. *Dapping blocks and punches* are used to form domes in metal. The block has machined hemispheric hollows of graduated sizes; when hammered, the complementary punches depress the metal into the hollow.

The scriber is a sharp, pencil-shaped tool used to mark metal for sawing and to texture metal surfaces.

A steel rule is used to measure or as a guide for scribing. Select a rule calibrated in both inches and metric measurement.

The burnisher is a polished, oval-shaped steel blade used for smoothing metal and curving bezels over stone settings.

Melting crucible and tongs are used for preparing and pouring molten silver in casting.

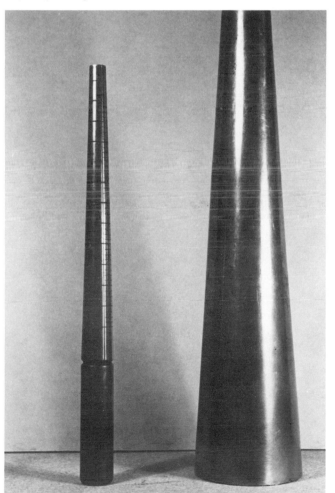

Ring mandrel and bracelet mandrel.

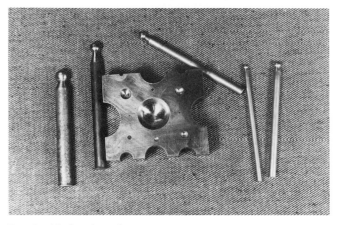

Dapping block and punches.

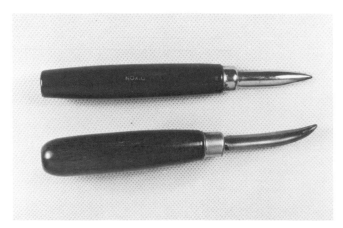

Straight and curved burnishers.

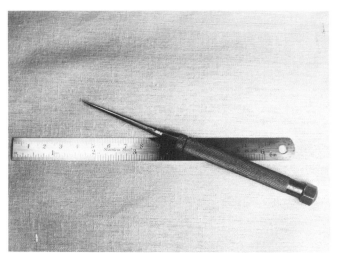

Scriber and steel rule.

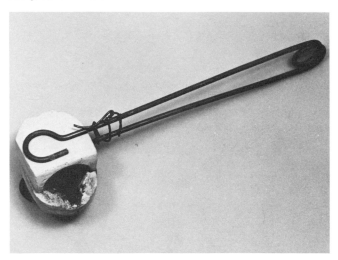

Melting crucible and holding tongs.

Soldering Equipment

Torches are available in a variety of designs. The author prefers the two described below because they are suited for both classroom and studio.

The Bernzomatic Bantam Torch is a small, self-contained propane hand torch well suited for small jewelry work. A full tank of fuel will fire for approximately fifteen hours and is replaceable.

The Prestolite Torch and Tank is a larger unit that can be equipped with different nozzle sizes to handle different operations.

An asbestos block protects the workbench from the torch flame during soldering. The block should be ½-inch (1.3 cm) thick and at least one foot square.

Small, self-contained propane torch.

Prestolite torch.

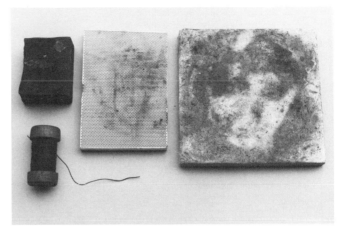

Charcoal block, ceramic soldering block, asbestos block, and soft iron binding wire.

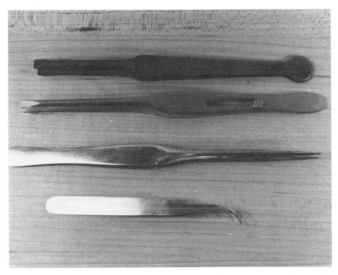

Tweezers. Top to bottom: soldering, slide-lock, pointed, and curved-point tweezers.

A **charcoal block** is used to hold the object being soldered. These blocks, which reflect heat back to the soldering point, are available in various sizes.

Soft iron wire is used to pin, clamp, and bind pieces of work for soldering.

Self-locking soldering tweezers hold pieces together during some soldering operations.

Pointed tweezers are used to move pieces of work into position for soldering.

Copper tongs should be used to handle hot metal and to immerse and remove metal from pickling solutions.

A **pickling container** is a heat-proof, deep glass tray used to hold silver cleaning solution. There are also commercial picklers with built in heating units.

Electric pickler.

Polishing Equipment

Polishing equipment may be no more than simple hand buffs and such polishing compounds as tripoli, pumice, and rouge. These compounds are a mixture of finely ground abrasives and a binder of wax. They are produced in easy-to-handle bars or ¼ pound sticks. However, an electric-powered polishing lathe equipped with tapered spindles and an assortment of buffs and compounds can aid in obtaining better results.

Some of the polishing wheels used with the electric buffing unit.

Electric powered buffing unit with a dust collecting hood.

Metals for Jewelry Making

Metal used in jewelry must be malleable. However, many metals temper (harden) as they are worked and require intermittent annealing (softening by heating) to restore their malleability.

Many metals polish to an excellent luster; silver and copper more so than brass or gold. Copper and brass tarnish rapidly and can discolor clothing and skin. To preserve their luster, copper and brass must be coated with clear lacquer.

Sterling silver, an alloy of 92½ percent silver and 7½ percent copper, is the metal used most often by jewelry makers. It is an excellent choice for the beginner.

Sterling silver is more costly than brass or copper, but it is worth the investment to produce a lasting piece of jewelry. Unless otherwise specified, the processes described in this book will be those for working with silver.

Silver may be purchased in may forms. Sheet silver comes in various gauges. The lower the gauge, the thicker the metal. For example, 20 gauge silver is .03196-inches (.8 mm) thick, 10 gauge silver is .10189-inches (2.6 mm) thick (refer to Appendix II for a comparison of gauges). Silver wire also comes in a variety of gauges and configurations — round, square, rectangular, triangular, half-round, low-dome.

The cost of silver sheet and wire is usually determined by weight. Most suppliers furnish listings of weight per inch or square inch for the various forms of silver, but dimension, rather than weight, is usually the better criterion for buying. An order for sheet silver should specify width, length, and gauge; one for silver wire should specify its cross-section, shape, gauge, and length.

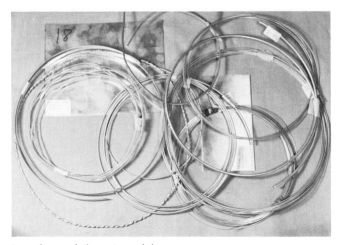

Some forms of silver wire and sheet.

Supplies

In addition to the tools and materials previously described, the following supplies should be acquired.

Silver Solder is used for silver, copper, and brass. Three grades are available: *easy* — flow point, 1325°F/718°C; *medium* — flow point, 1390°F/754°C; *hard* — flow point, 1450°F/788°C. On projects requiring multiple soldering steps, the higher flow point solder is used first, then the lower flow point solder. All grades are available in either sheet or wire form. The former is recommended.

Hard soldering flux is applied to both metal and solder to keep their surfaces clean and to prevent oxides from forming during heating.

Cleaning and pickling solutions. Sparex No. 2 and Pre-Po Pickle are recommended for the cleaning and pickling processes that remove metal oxides that form during soldering. These solutions are much safer than commercial acids.

Polishing compounds and oxidants are required for specific uses and are listed in the chapter on surface treatment.

Beeswax is available in block form and lubricates the jeweler's saw blade during cutting.

Powdered borax is used as a flux in silver casting.

Yellow ochre is mixed with water to provide a heat shield for soldered joints.

Scotch stone is a soft, slatelike stone that is used with water to remove blemishes from hard to reach surfaces.

The tools, materials, and supplies listed in this chapter are considered basic equipment for jewelry making. Some additional items mentioned in later chapters will be needed only for specific processes or techniques.

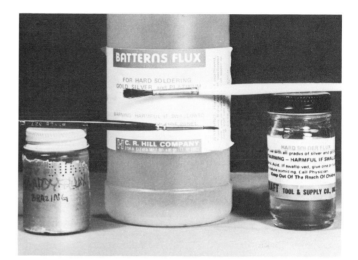
Soldering fluxes and brushes used for applying flux.

Pre-Po Pickle and Sparex No. 2.

Yellow ochre.

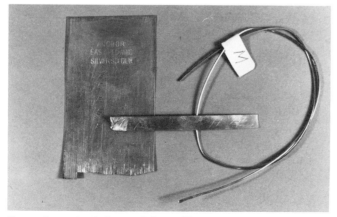
Sheet, wire, and strip forms of silver solder.

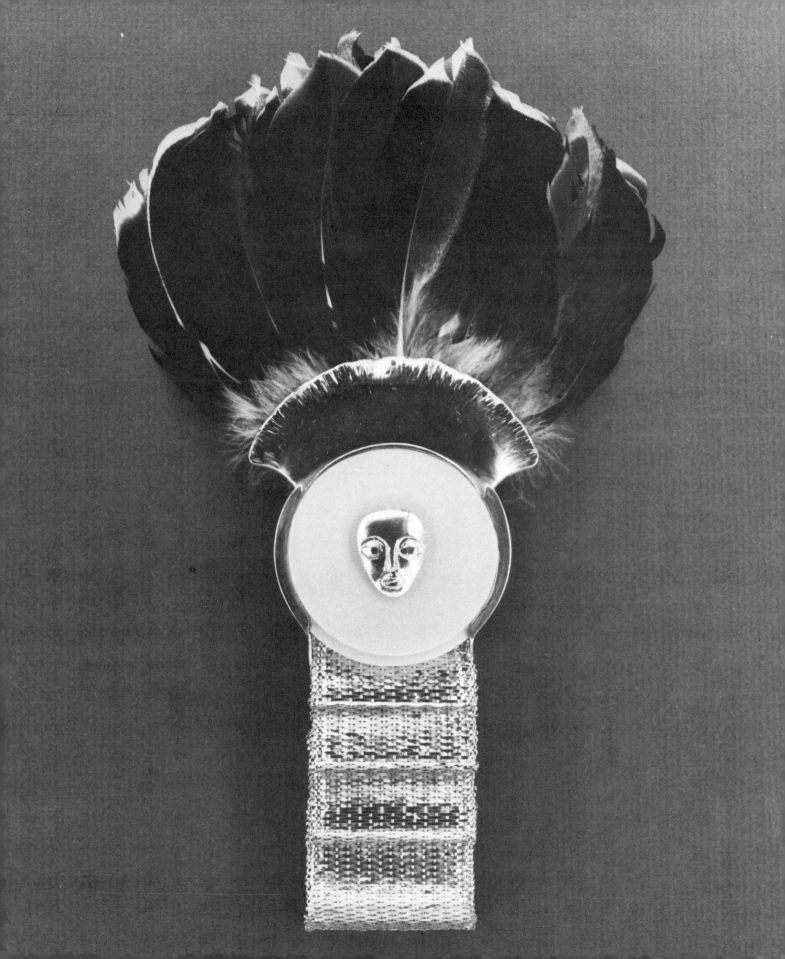

CHAPTER 2

*Design
&
Craftsmanship*

above: *Choker #34* by Mary Lee Hu, 1977. Fine silver, sterling silver, 14K gold, 24K gold, wrapped and looped. This choker is an example of symmetrically balanced design. Its dynamism results from its varied and related flowing line rhythms and the sensitive placement of forms and textures.

left: Fan/brooch by Arline M. Fisch, 1977. Sterling silver construction, ivory, chased silver face, woven fine silver handle and feathers mounted separately. 9″ (22.9 cm) high, 4½″ (11.4 cm) wide. This exquisitely designed brooch is a fine example of the interest created by varying surfaces and textures.

Jewelry making requires an equal regard for both design and construction skills. Success in jewelry making depends upon how effectively one can orchestrate process and technical skills with appropriate materials and still maintain an effective application of the elements and principles of design.

Teachers and texts can stifle learners with formal, rule-laden approaches to designing with materials. Design awareness is a perception process that evolves from a penetrating and thoughtful observation of one's world.

Analyze the environment. Identify the visual elements of line, shape and form, color and value, texture and space. Learn how balance, unity, emphasis, rhythm, and contrast give expression to the visual elements and establish order.

Elements of Design

The elements of design have distinct characteristics:

LINE

With your eyes and hands, follow the lines occurring in the environment. Notice their variety — short, long, thick, thin, straight, curved, irregular; how they create movement and mood; how they establish direction and form shapes; how they develop rhythms. Are there combinations of lines visible that create textures or add details to shapes?

SHAPE AND FORM

Our world offers an infinite variety of shapes and forms. Shapes are two dimensional and may be classified as geometric (oval, circular, triangular, square, or rectangular) or organic (irregular or amorphous). *Form* is three dimensional and results when planes add depth to width and height.

Become aware of the multitude of shapes and forms that you see. Analyze how designers, artists, and craftspersons use shape and form to create pattern, texture, movement, mood, contrast and how they establish unity and balance. Study the unique shapes and forms that occur in natural objects.

COLOR AND VALUE

Colors are associated with many of our feelings. Color is a psychological stimulator that establishes mood, evokes mystery, induces calm, and sparks excitement. The world around us is filled with color and color combinations. Examine the role color plays in advertising, fashion, television, the arts, the crafts, and in the many products and activities that are a part of our lives. Observe how color is used to create form, shape, texture and to establish unity, balance, movement, and mood.

Value is the relative lightness or darkness of a color or

A silhouetted basketball net. The contained irregular lines of the hoop and support add interest to the off-center inner circle.

This piece of driftwood is a fluid, unified design of lines that have created shapes, textures, and rhythms.

Lines create movement, forms, and textures in this fragment of a gold Manchu ornamental headdress. Notice how the rhythmic line movement resembles the structuring in Chinese painting. Ming Dynasty, 1368–1664 A.D. The Metropolitan Museum of Art, New York, Rogers Fund, 1929.

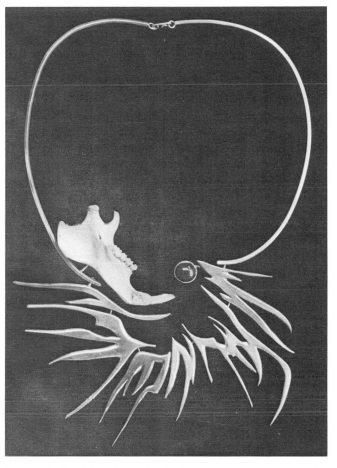

Necklace by Carol Anspach, 1978. Sterling silver with the jawbone of a woodchuck. Exciting movement and tension are created by the shapes in this necklace. Notice how the forms direct one's vision to the gemstone. Photograph by Ed Sachs.

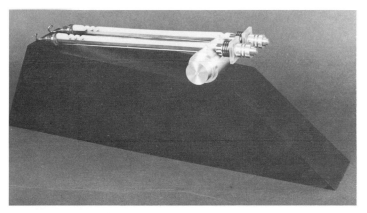

Brooch # 6.2 by David W. Keens. Brass, acrylic, aluminum, black anodized aluminum, and enamel paints. The bold, direct forms in this brooch lend a smooth, visual movement to the carefully planned contrasting surfaces and shapes.

The random compacting of river gravel produces a static design from a variety of massed forms and shapes. Focus is on the single, contrasting, dark pebble.

A recently sawed tree stump covered with sawdust, chips, and tree sap becomes a composition suggesting the energy and excitement of a Jackson Pollack painting.

Stacked concrete blocks produce a contrasting, powerful shadow pattern against a plane of various textures.

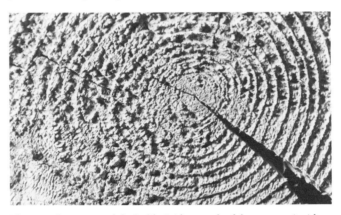

The rugged texture and the bold, rigid strength of the concentric ridges in this log are contrasted and opposed by the developing cracks.

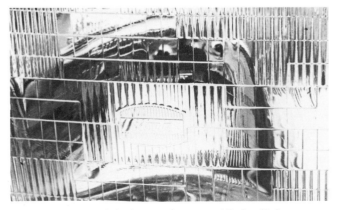

The tonal range and the lines in an automobile headlight weave a dynamic and mysterious composition.

The dark spaces between the louvers of a door combine with the shadow pattern of a nearby railing to create an interesting composition with an irregular rhythm pattern.

surface. Value can be used to define forms and it plays an important part in defining shapes.

TEXTURE

The surface quality of an object evokes specific psychological and physical sensations peculiar to that texture. These sensations may be visual or tactile. Through experience, we learn to distinguish between such surfaces as hard-soft, slick-rough, jagged-smooth and to appreciate the subtleties between extremes.

Surface textures are designed to inspire interest, establish mood, create visual contrasts, develop unity, and provide balance. Glance around. Are many diffferent textures visible? How might they be described? What feelings do they evoke?

SPACE

Study the open areas around and between objects and notice how these spaces affect the relationship between the objects. Observe how space on the pages of this book serves to emphasize the illustrations and to create a sense of balance and unity within each page.

Artists, designers, and craftspersons use space to establish relationships and scale, to create movement and rhythm, and to achieve balance and unity.

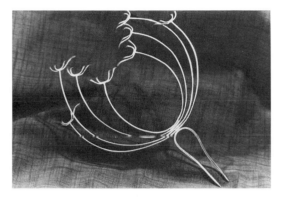

Hair ornament by Clara Schlegel. 14K yellow gold, constructed and forged. The varying spaces between the units of this piece give emphasis and establish balanced unity. Photograph by Larry Langdon.

Principles of Design

Together, the visual elements of design form the basis for all we see. The organization of these elements is achieved through the application of certain design principles — balance, unity, movement, rhythm, pattern, emphasis, and contrast.

BALANCE

Balance is the equalization of forces. A design is balanced when the qualities of the components present a visual equalization. Visual balance is categorized as *symmetrical, asymmetrical,* and *radial*.

Symmetrical or *formal balance* occurs when the elements are identical on both sides of a central axis. Symmetrical balance imparts a sense of strength and solidity. Common examples include the architecture of colonial homes, many churches and office buildings.

Asymmetrical or *informal balance* achieves balance and stability through visual equalization of the design elements. Many artists and craftspersons utilize asymmetrical balance because of its dynamic potential.

In *radial balance*, the design elements radiate outward from a central point much like the spokes in a wheel. Radial designs convey a sense of stability and completeness.

The eye-catching translucent seed pods of lunaria (money plant) surround a delicately balanced asymmetrical grouping of seeds that appear as dots and lines.

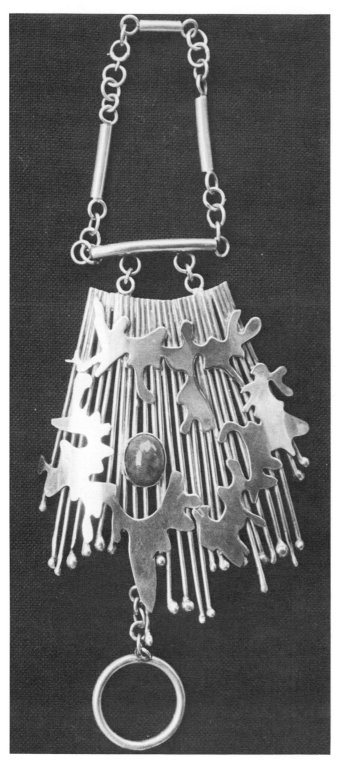

Hand ornament by Carol Anspach. Sterling silver with lapis lazuli. The ring slips over the finger and the barred chain encircles the wrist. Visual equalization of the elements in this asymmetrical design establishes unity and stability. Photograph by Ed Sachs.

This shasta daisy is an example of radial design. Notice the moving optical effect created by the varying sizes of the spheres in the center disk of the flower.

UNITY

Unity brings a sense of oneness to a design. The elements appear to belong together; their placement integrates them into the wholeness of the design.

MOVEMENT AND RHYTHM

Placing related elements in a series creates movement and rhythm. Repeated shapes and continuing lines lead a viewer's eyes through space. Movement and rhythm can flow or throb, race with excitement, swirl with mystery.

PATTERN

Pattern develops when similar design units are repeated within a space. Because pattern is based upon repetition, it is inherently rhythmic. Wallpaper and floor tile are examples of formal patterns whose rhythm is even and regular. A field of flowers or an autumn ground cover of fallen leaves is an example of informal pattern with an irregular and exciting rhythm.

EMPHASIS

Emphasis is achieved by stressing an element or series of elements in a design. Shape, size, color, value, texture, and line can all be used to stress the visual importance of a particular area in a design.

CONTRAST

Contrast means difference or opposition. Contrasting elements in a design lend variety and arouse interest by offering visual comparisons. Contrast is often used to achieve emphasis.

An awareness of these basic elements and principles of design expands your ability to observe. Many craftspersons use a sketchbook to record their observations and interpretations and later find their sketches to be a valuable resource for ideas in jewelry designing.

The linear vein pattern of the plantain lily leaves are symmetrical. However, the grouping of the leaves in this photograph is asymmetrical. Notice how the center leaf is emphasized by the shadow patterns.

The utility pole and the clustered forms attached to it are emphasized by size, tonal value, and line movement.

The end-grain lines and textures of piled landscaping timbers display an unusual variety of interesting patterns.

Practicality of Design

Jewelry has a uniqueness as an art form because its function is to adorn the body. This singleness of function does not limit the designer's creativity, but it does require a regard for several practical considerations.

Wearability. Jewelry should be free from jagged and sharp edges that could cut, scratch, or snag.

Weight and size. The weight and size of jewelry should suit the wearer. Rings and bracelets should feel comfortable; earrings and pendants should not burden the wearer.

Balance. Pins, pendants, and earrings should hang properly and feel comfortable.

Durability. The jewelry material should be durable. Its finish should be easy to maintain.

Security. Findings, catches, and fastening devices should hold securely and be durable.

These practical considerations are important factors in designing jewelry and are related to its use and appearance. Jewelry that functions only in a display case has not been properly designed.

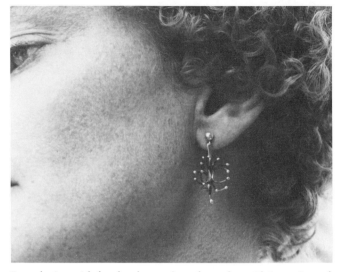

Round wires with fused ends were bound together with iron wire and then cluster soldered at their midpoints to create this earring. Several snippets of solder were placed between each of the wires to ensure a strong bond.

Experimenting with Metal

If jewelry making is your first experience with metal, some experimentation with soft metals will help you to appreciate their potentials and limitations. Copper and brass foil, sheeting, and wire are excellent materials for experimentation. So is heavy aluminum foil.

Try bending narrow strips of sheet metal by hand or with pliers. Place the metal on a corner of a wooden block or dowel and pound it with a wooden mallet. Notice the effect on metal when it is pounded with a ball-peened hammer on a steel block. Try different hammers. Try texturing metal with a nail set and punches. Scratch it with a scriber.

Bend wire with pliers. Pound it on a steel block. Try combinations of bending and pounding. Notice the changes that occur in shape and texture. Feel how the wire stiffens and hardens when it is manipulated.

Loop wire through holes that have been drilled in a thin sheet of metal. Try to arrange the pieces into a design that is unified and interesting.

Such experimentation will provide the beginning jewelry maker with a feel for metal, an essential part of jewelry making.

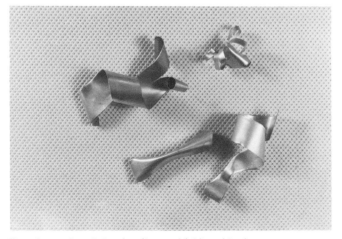

Experiments in twisting, bending, and folding thin sheet copper.

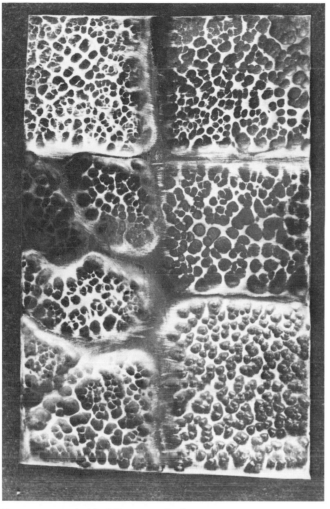

Textures created with different peening hammers.

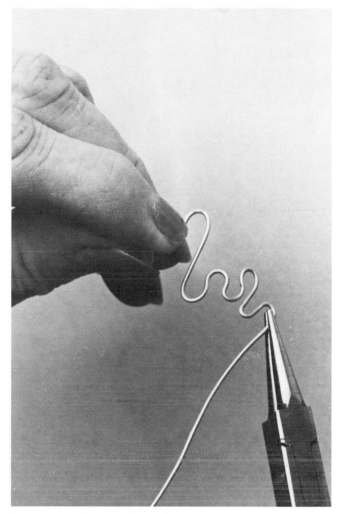

Experiment with wire and round nose pliers to develop interesting forms, shapes, and rhythms.

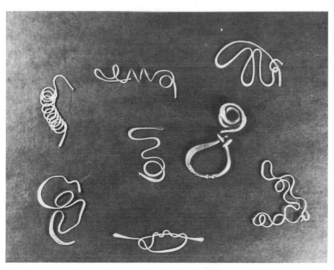

Experimental pieces of twisted and pounded wire.

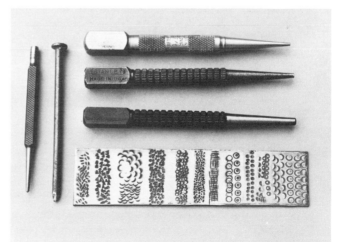

Textures created with nail sets, center punch, and a common nail.

Developing Designs

There are a number of methods that might be used to develop a jewelry design.

When fashion designers develop a design they *sketch* many roughs called *croquis*. The croquis approach is excellent for jewelry designing because it allows the designer to explore many variations on a basic idea. As the design evolves, continually evaluate it in these terms:

• Can the design be translated into jewelry materials?
• Can it be constructed with the available tools and materials?
• Does the design meet the practical requirements of jewelry?
• Does it possess visual unity, interest, and completeness?

MODELING WITH FOIL AND PAPER

File cards, heavy paper, and heavy aluminum foil can be cut, folded, bent, and twisted to form a model of the jewelry design. Again, explore many variations of an idea, because experimentation will stimulate the development of design awareness and fluency.

As your design capability grows, the need for elaborate sketch work diminishes. The jewelry maker may even prefer to eliminate this intermediate step and *design directly* with the jewelry material.

Regardless of the development approach you use, the central idea should remain open to adaptation and refinement, because tools, materials, and the working process itself often inspire more provocative results.

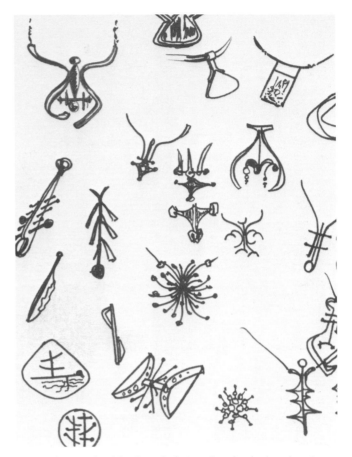

A page from a sketchbook with design ideas for further thought or development.

Sources for Design Ideas

Our world is filled with unlimited sources for design ideas — the earth, sea, sky, manufactured and natural forms. Nonobjective designs suggested by the manipulation of jewelry materials and the potential these materials embrace for surface variations offer exciting possibilities. This spontaneous creativity typifies the approach of many contemporary jewelry makers.

Try to expand your thinking about what jewelry is and what jewelry should be. Compare and contrast contemporary jewelry with that from the past. Visit museums, galleries, craft shows, and shops. Look through books and catalogs. Examine the jewelry you see for design quality, effective use of materials, construction techniques, and finishing methods.

When you have searched your environment, the heritage of human history, and your inner-most self for ideas, decide what you like and why you like it. Then, with your materials and techniques, express your individuality and your values. Demonstrate your creativity and craftsmanship through the originality of your own designs.

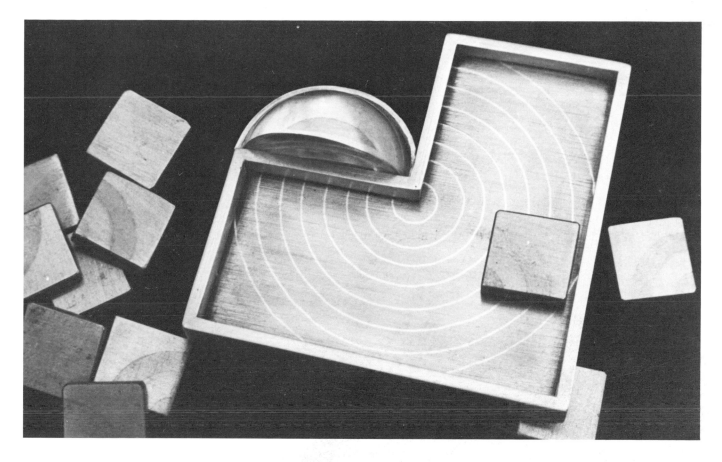

above: Geometric brooch by Deborah F. Love Jemmott. Brooch and table piece. Sterling silver, nickel silver, brass, acrylic, spring steel, 2½" × 2½" × 1" (6.4 cm × 6.4 cm × 2.5 cm). The nickel silver back plate is inlaid with sterling silver. The frame and the pinback are sterling. The acrylic hemisphere lens covers a married metal half-circle of silver and nickel silver. The square puzzle parts are brass and nickel silver, laminated on brass. By varying the positions of the squares within the frame, many rhythmic designs can be improvised.

left: Gold jewelry from ancient Peruvian tombs. Courtesy of The American Museum of Natural History, New York.

CHAPTER 3

Cutting, Drilling
&
Filing

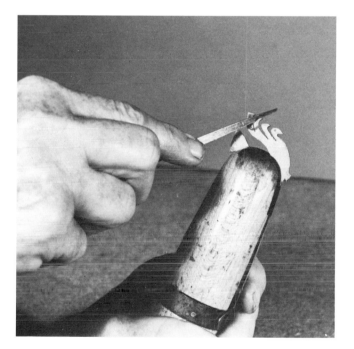

above: Small, intricate shapes can be held steady in a ring clamp.

left: Drilling with a pin-vise.

Once the design is finalized and the appropriate materials are selected, the actual process of creating the piece begins. Keep in mind the considerations of durability and practicality. Generally, rings and bracelets are made from sheet silver in B & S gauge 12, 14, or 16, and lightweight pierced designs and pendants from gauge 18. Pins, ear- rings, beads, buttons, and stone mounting bezels are made from sheet gauges 18 to 26, the larger pieces requiring the heavier material. Silver wire in gauges 4 to 14 is suitable for forging. The wire chosen should be thick enough to retain the shape of the original design.

Transferring the Design to Metal

Before sheet silver is cut, the jewelry design must first be scribed into the metal. There are three different ways to do this:

• Draw or trace a fine line on the metal with a pencil. Then, lightly incise the line with a fine pointed scriber. If changes are needed later, lightly scribed lines are easier to remove. Use a metal rule as a guide to scribe straight lines.

• Cut a pattern of the design from index cards and carefully scribe around the pattern on the metal.

• Cut the design from paper and rubber cement it to the metal.

Place the design on the silver sheet so waste is minimized. Handle the sheet with care to prevent scratches and marks that may be difficult to remove later.

A design drawn on paper and cemented to sheet metal can serve as a layout for cutting with the jeweler's saw. Note how the design was located on the sheet to minimize the cutting.

Cutting

CUTTING WITH SNIPS

Strips of metal can be cut with tinner's snips or aviation snips. Both tools crimp, however, and are not suited for intricate cutting. Always cut outside the scribed line so crimping can be filed away.

Jeweler's snips can be used to cut thin sheet silver (24 gauge or lighter). Again, cut outside the scribed line so that the edge can be restored by filing.

CUTTING WIRE

Heavy jewelry wire, 14 gauge or thicker, should be cut with the jeweler's saw; thinner wire should be cut with nippers. File the cut ends of the wire to remove the peaks formed by the nipper's blades.

CUTTING WITH THE JEWELER'S SAW

The jeweler's saw is one of the essential tools in jewelry

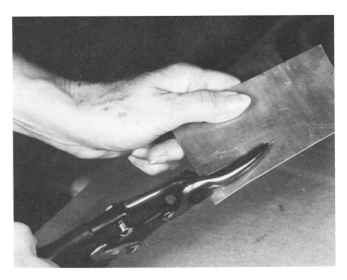

Cutting a strip of sheet metal with aviation snips.

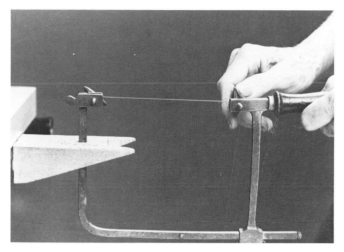

A method for bracing the jeweler's saw to establish blade tension.

Close-up of the jeweler's saw blade showing proper angle of teeth.

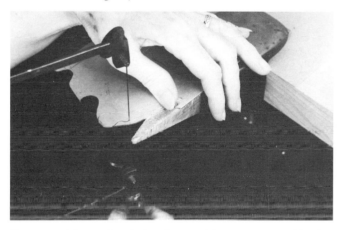

Placement of the metal on the bench pin and the proper saw position for cutting sheet metal.

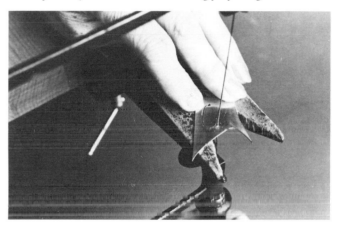

Making a pierced cut in a sheet silver form with the jeweler's saw. Note the drilled hole that is needed to insert the saw blade.

making. Mastering it is important. It is the only tool that can be used to accurately cut small, intricate shapes and lines.

Use a blade in the mid-range size of No. 1 to 2/0. Handle the blade carefully because it is fragile and brittle. To load the blade in the saw:

• Loosen the clamps on both ends of the saw frame.

• Insert the blade all the way into the top clamp (the clamp opposite the handle end) with the teeth pointing away from the frame and angled toward the handle. (Cutting occurs on the downstroke.) Tighten the top clamp when the blade is aligned with the handle clamp.

• If necessary, adjust the frame so the unattached blade end is within 1/8-inch (3 mm) of the handle clamp.

• Place the end of the frame against the workbench. Push the handle toward the unfastened blade end until the blade is about 1/2-inch (1.3 cm) inside the clamp. Tighten the clamp and gently relax the pushing pressure.

• Pluck the blade with a fingernail. A high pitched ping indicates proper tension.

• Lubricate the blade lightly with beeswax. Too much wax will clog the teeth. Remove any excess wax.

When the saw is ready, place the metal so the inscribed design rests over the cutout (v) in the bench pin. *The saw blade must be kept in a vertical position at all times,* otherwise it will break. Move the saw gently up and down to start the cut. Proceed slowly with complete strokes. Do not force the blade forward or downward; it will naturally feed into the metal as cutting proceeds. Allowing the blade to drift away from a vertical position will invariably result in a broken blade.

When a cornering or angling cut is required, cut to the turning point, and move the blade up and down without forward motion while gently turning the saw frame to the new direction.

For curved cuts, guide the blade along the line with light pressure, or, if preferred, keep the saw in one cutting position and move the metal to attain the desired cut. With experience you will develop a cutting technique that best suits your needs.

To back out of a cut, work gently and slowly. Force could cause a pinching action which will snap the blade. If the blade will not back out of a cut, release one clamp and pull the blade through the cut.

Sawing is a skill essential to jewelry making. The time spent to develop that skill is well invested.

PIERCED CUTS WITH THE JEWELER'S SAW

Cutting an open shape from the design's interior requires a procedure called *piercing*. Place the metal on a bench block. On the inner, or *waste side*, where the opening is to be made, mark a spot for drilling with a center punch. Drill through the metal with a small bit, No. 58 or 60. Remove the lower blade end from the saw and thread it through the drilled hole. Be certain that the design surface is facing upward, away from the handle. Reclamp the blade and complete the piercing cut with the metal supported on the bench pin. Remove the blade by drawing it back through the metal.

Drilling

Drilling holes, a basic operation in jewelry making, is a relatively simple operation. Always mark the location for drilling with a center punch so that the spinning bit will not drift and cause scratches. Before drilling, secure the metal in a smooth-jawed vise, using a back-up block of wood or with small nails driven into a wood block. This prevents the metal from spinning as the drill bit turns.

The back-up wood supports the metal and also helps to make a cleaner cut.

Always remember to tighten bits securely in the drill chuck and to use light pressure with small bits.

Very small bits should be used in a pin vise. Protect the bit by exposing only enough of it to pierce the metal.

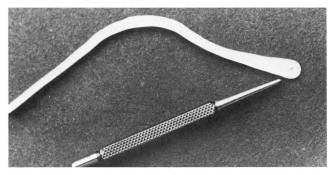

The center punch marks the location for drilling a hole. The indentation made by the punch will steady the drill tip and prevent its drifting.

Drilling punch-marked holes with a hand drill on a back-up block of wood. The small nails prevent the piece from spinning from the motion of the drill bit.

Filing and Smoothing

Cutting causes rough and irregular edges on metal. Files are used to smooth and refine these edges.

The piece to be filed should be held in a smooth-jawed vise, ring clamp, or hand-braced against the bench pin. The ring clamp is a versatile device that can hold objects at any desired working angle. Accurate filing is possible

only when the object is held in a firm and steady position.

A No. 2 cut flat, 6-inch (15.2 cm) file effectively smooths straight edges and convex curves. The curved side of a No. 2 cut half-round file should be used for smoothing concave edge forms.

Small, intricate areas in designs can be smoothed with

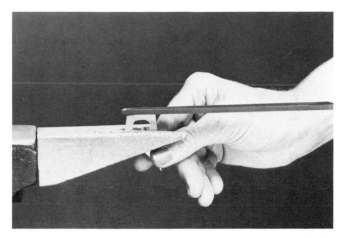

Edge filing using the bench pin to help firmly brace the metal. The file should be kept parallel to the surface being smoothed.

needle files, which are available in assorted shapes and sizes. Best results will be obtained when the shape of the file's cutting edge most closely matches the contour of the edge being filed.

Riffle files are made in various shapes to be used for areas inaccessible to needle files. They are excellent for removing excess solder from joints and for smoothing concaved shapes.

All files cut on the forward stroke (away from the body). Pressure should be released on the back stroke to prevent unnecessary dulling.

The finer the cut of a file, the sooner it will clog requiring cleaning with a file card or stiff bristle brush.

Do not use jewelry files on lead or lead solder. Lead left on a file can contaminate silver and cause pitting when the silver is heated.

Reclaiming Cutting Waste and Filings

Cutting, drilling, and filing produce scrap pieces and particles of metal that should be saved. Cutting waste can often be used in the development of a design. Scrap silver can be used for fused constructions or melted for casting operations.

All silver scrap, including the tiniest particles, should be reclaimed. Waste not suitable for fusing or casting can be sold to precious metals dealers.

Some professional jewelers' workbenches are equipped with a tray, located under the bench pin, to catch small particles of metal. A similar system can be devised by clamping a rectangular plastic pan to the bench or by placing the pan on a waste basket under the bench pin.

The small particles of silver grated off by saws and files can be used for creating fused surface textures or casting, but only after they are pickled. To clean this type of scrap prior to pickling:

• Place the filings on a large piece of paper and remove any ferrous metal, such as bits of saw blades, with a magnet.

• Put the filings in an iron skillet and heat them on a stove until all organic matter, such as wood and paper, are burned off.

• Cool, then cover the filings with water. When the burned organic material floats on top of the water, carefully pour the water off and allow the filings to dry.

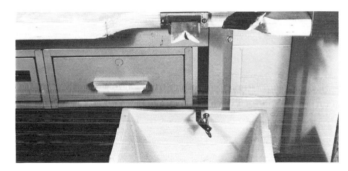

A plastic wash pan clamped under the bench pin will catch filings and cuttings of valuable metals.

Salt and Pepper Shakers with Teaball, neckpiece by Deborah E. Love Jemmott, 1977. Sterling silver with green and orange acrylic fabricated.

CHAPTER 4

Joining & Fastening with Solder

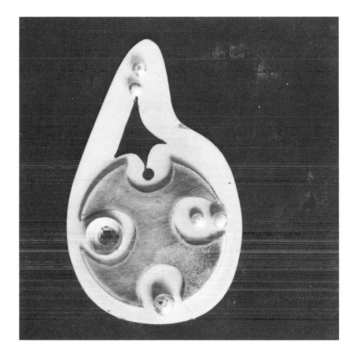

above: Section with the premelted solder positioned for soldering. Sphere units and bezel will be soldered at the same time. Joint is complete when the solder shows as a glistening line between the two pieces.

left: Bracelet by John T. Fix. Sterling silver set with onyx. Fix describes the construction: "The larger element is about ¾″ (1.9 cm) square and is a hollow fabrication. The smaller element is a solid forging. The pieces are hinged underneath and held closed with a box catch." Photograph by Mark Habicht.

Soldering techniques can be mastered by following some basic rules.

Fitting

Good soldering requires close fittings along the line of contact. Solder will not fill gaps or cover up careless workmanship.

Butt-end soldering (joining wire or metal end to end), such as jump rings, ring, bezel, and bracelet ends, requires a perfect fit. File the ends of the pieces to be joined so that no gaps exist when the edges are brought together. Perpendicular additions to flat areas require the same precise fit.

Flat surfaces to be joined should not be dented or warped. If dents or warps exist, place the item bulge up on a smooth, hard surface, such as a steel bench block, and hammer them out with a rawhide mallet.

Cleaning

Because solder will not flow on dirty surfaces, the contact areas must be completely clean. Surfaces can be cleaned in a number of ways:

• Lightly rub the contact areas with emery paper (No. 400) until the surface is bright. Avoid deep scratches.

• With fingers or brush, rub the area with moistened pumice powder.

• Immerse the pieces in a warm Sparex No. 2 pickling solution for four or five minutes.

Silver necklace with antique spider webs and spiders by Carol Anspach. Skillful soldering was essential in the construction of this necklace. Photograph by Ed Sachs.

Fluxing

Fluxing prevents oxidation that occurs when metal is heated. Solder will not flow on or adhere to an oxidized surface. Before soldering, apply flux with a small sable brush to both joining areas and to the solder. After use, rinse the brush in water to prevent a flux buildup that could damage the bristles.

Handy Flux is a borax-based paste effective with silver and copper alloy metals. Many commercial self-pickling liquid fluxes are also available. Always follow the manufacturer's directions and always provide for adequate ventilation when soldering because flux releases toxic fumes.

Solder and Solder Preparation

Sheet metal and wire can be joined by using either soft or hard solder. The use of soft solder, composed of lead and tin with a melting point of about 400°F (204°C), in jewelry making is limited primarily to the fastening of findings (connecting devices) that cannot withstand high heat.

Hard solder, also called silver solder, is used universally by jewelry makers for joining silver. The proportion of the metals — silver, copper and zinc — used in the alloy process determines the melting and flow point of the solder. It comes in graded designations for specific melting points:

Solder Designation	Melting Point	Flow Point
Easy	1260°F/682°C	1325°F/718°C
Medium	1335°F/724°C	1390°F/754°C
Hard	1435°F/779°C	1450°F/788°C

Another silver solder, usually designated *very easy* and with a melting point of 1175°F (635°C), is not recommended for classroom use because it often contains cadmium. Cadmium solder releases fumes that are extremely dangerous.

In complex jewelry requiring a series of soldering operations, the hard, or highest melting point solder, is used first; each successive soldering is done with the next lower grade. For almost all simple soldering, however, the easy grade is adequate.

Silver solder is available in sheets, strips, wire, and precut pieces. For classroom and studio use, the strip or sheet form is ideal. It is helpful to identify newly purchased solder by scratching in an E, M, or H at one-inch intervals. Solder should be thinner than the metals being joined — this assures adequate heat transfer. A 28 or 30 gauge solder usually satisfies that requirement.

To prepare sheet and strip solder for use, clean it on both sides with fine emery paper and cut it into small pieces, commonly called snippets. Make a series of parallel cuts with the jeweler's snips at 1 mm (1/32-inch to 1/16-inch) intervals across the end of the solder sheet. Then, from the side of the sheet, snip across the original cuts at right angles to form 1 mm square snippets.

Snippets will adhere well to a fine brush moistened with flux and can be transferred to the soldering point with the brush or with fine tweezers.

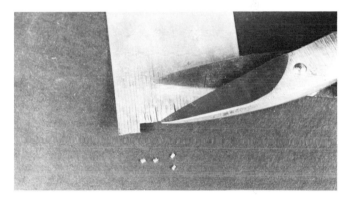

Solder snippets are prepared by snipping across parallel cuts made in sheet solder.

Soldering Torches

The small propane torch — the Bernzomatic Bantam — is adequate for making small jewelry. The acetylene unit is better for prolonged studio use and for making large jewelry. (Classrooms and studios equipped with built-in gas-air torch systems require neither of these units.)

Both units automatically blend the fuel with air and provide for varying the flame length. Tips come in many sizes that produce a variety of flames, but for most jewelry work a No. 1 tip is a good selection.

The gas-air torch units installed in some schools and workshops allow the proportion of compressed air to gas to be varied. Too much gas in this mixture results in an amorphous yellow flame that deposits soot. Too much air produces a dark blue, hard-pointed flame that forms oxides that prevent solder from flowing. The proper fuel mixture burns in a four- or five-inch flame with a light blue center cone surrounded by a darker blue outer cone, with a trace of yellow in a gently flaring flame tip. The hottest spot in the flame occurs at a point beyond the tip of the inner cone and near the center of the outer cone.

A torch flame showing the inner and outer cones.

Use caution when lighting any torch. The torch tip should always be pointed away from the operator. Hold a lighted match at the mouth of the torch tip, then open the fuel valve only slightly until ignition occurs. Gradually advance the valve control until the desired flame size is reached. The air control on the gas-air torch should not be opened until after the torch has ignited. After soldering, tightly close the valve(s) on the torch. Always follow the directions that accompany the torch.

Because effective soldering requires careful observation of the changing color of the metal being heated, soldering should be done under subdued light or in a dark area. The following color-temperature indicators for silver can be used as a guide:

Faint red	approx. 900°F (482°C)	
Dull red	approx. 1200°F (649°C)	Handy Flux melts
Red	approx. 1325°F (718°C)	Easy solder flows
Light red	approx. 1390°F (754°C)	Medium solder flows
Orange	approx. 1450°F (788°C)	Hard solder flows
Red orange	approx. 1640°F (893°C)	Sterling silver melts

Note that the temperature difference between the melting point of flux and the melting point of silver is only 440°F. The need for careful observation is obvious.

Pickling

The pickling process removes the oxides that form on the surface of the metal. The heat used in soldering causes these oxides to form rapidly.

The pickling solution commonly used in jewelry making is a 10 percent solution of sulphuric acid (1 part acid to 10 parts of water). TO MAKE THIS SOLUTION SAFELY, ALWAYS ADD ACID TO WATER. However, because concentrated acids and acid solutions are so dangerous to use and store in classrooms and studios, safer substitutes are available. Sparex No. 2, a commercially-prepared pickle for nonferrous metals, is recommended for school use. Sparex No. 2 is a granular preparation packaged in 10 ounce and 2½ pound containers. It is mixed with water according to the directions provided. Ten ounces will make 1 quart of pickle; 2½ pounds will make one gallon.

Sparex is a corrosive substance which can cause burns. *Follow the directions and cautions printed on the label.* All pickling solutions should be used with adequate ventilation. Do not breathe the fumes created when hot metal is placed in the solution.

A heat-resistant, deep Pyrex dish with a lid is recommended as a pickling and storage container for Sparex. Copper tongs must be used to remove objects from the pickle. Ferrous metal in any form — iron binding wires, tools — contaminates the solution. Jewelry may be

Copper tongs are used to remove objects from the pickle solution.

placed in the pickling solution while it is hot (as described in the section on soldering), but avoid splashing by gently submerging the piece with copper tongs. If the place to be treated is cool, the pickling solution should be heated to 140°F (60°C). An electric pickle pot that maintains a constant pickling temperature is excellent for treating cold objects.

Silver should be left in the solution until it whitens. When this occurs, remove the piece and rinse thoroughly with water.

When the solution discolors or fails to clean effectively, it should be discarded.

Work Surface for Soldering

A workbench should be protected with about a square foot of asbestos board. A charcoal block, centered on the asbestos, is used as the soldering surface. Charcoal retains heat and radiates some of it back to the soldering point. A piece being soldered can be held in place by surrounding it with several pins or wires stuck into the charcoal.

The Soldering Operation

The following section covers the basic techniques for soldering, but they can be adapted to your own construction needs.

SWEAT SOLDERING

Sweat soldering is used to join surfaces of flat metal. The pieces should be smooth and clean and they should fit precisely.

With a small brush apply flux to the contact surfaces and to every snippet needed. The flux must completely cover the contact areas, because solder will flow only on fluxed areas. Using a small brush that has been dipped in flux, place snippets at intervals of no more than 3/16-inch (4-5 mm) on the back of the piece that will cover the other.

Place the bottom piece with its fluxed side up on the charcoal block. Allow the flux holding the snippets on the top piece to partially dry, then carefully invert the piece and place it in position on the bottom one. With careful handling, the flux will hold the snippets in position.

Allow the flux to air dry, then gently heat the piece with the tip of the torch's outer flame to complete the drying. Heat very slowly because sudden high heat will cause the flux to bubble vigorously and shift or blow the solder out of position.

After the flux has dried (it will have a dull crusty appearance), begin heating the larger bottom piece from the outer edge and work the flame inward toward the top piece. Bring both pieces to the melting point of the solder. The heat and color of the metal should be uniform on all surfaces.

When the solder melts and flows — it will appear as a glistening line between the two pieces — remove the

above left: Solder fluxed and positioned for premelting prior to sweat soldering to a base.

above right: Partially melted solder. The piece has been pickled and will be refluxed, then placed solder side down on the fluxed base.

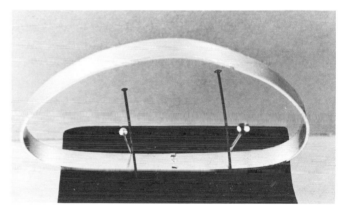

Solder positioned for butt soldering bracelet ends together. Pins are used to hold the piece in position on the charcoal soldering block.

Solder joint, after cleaning and light filing, is not visible.

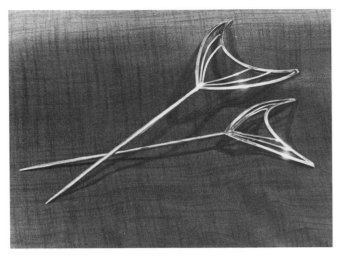

Hair ornaments by Clara Schlegel. 14K gold, constructed by soldering, then forged. Photograph by Larry Langdon.

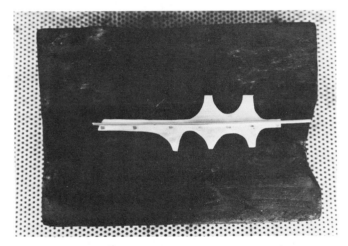

Solder placement for fastening a round wire to a flat surface. Torch flame will be applied from the left side.

Edge soldering square wire to a fused form. Solder is placed so that it touches both pieces. Pins hold the wires in position on the charcoal block.

flame. Allow the soldered piece to cool for a minute, then pickle it to remove the oxides. When the silver whitens, remove it and rinse in clean water.

An alternative method of sweat soldering overlaid pieces is to premelt the solder on the underside of the top piece before it is placed in position. Heat the piece only until the solder begins to melt. Overheating will reduce the solder's flowing ability. After the solder is melted, pickle, dry, and reflux the top piece. This method works well for small pieces and eliminates the possibility of snippets shifting.

SOLDERING BUTT SEAMS AND JOINTS

Butt seams and joints are formed when ring or bracelet ends are brought together, when sheets are joined, and when the ends of wires and tubes are connected. As in all soldering, the fit must be exact and the surfaces must be clean.

Apply flux along and into the joint. Place fluxed snippets at 1/8-inch (3 mm) intervals across the seam so that they touch both pieces. Heat slowly, moving the flame uniformly over the entire piece. When the solder flows into the seam, remove the heat and pickle the piece.

Pegs, pins, and the placement of some jewelry findings require butt soldering operations that may necessitate special holding techniques. This is covered in Chapters 7 and 9.

SOLDERING WIRES ON SHEETS

Be sure there is good contact between the sheet and the wire. Clean and flux the contact areas. Place the snippets at least 1-inch (2.5 cm) apart on 18 to 20 gauge wire. They should touch both the wire and the flat piece. When soldering wire with tight curves, place the snippets on the outside of the curve so that any blemish left by the solder can be more easily removed by a scraper or file.

Begin heating by concentrating the flame on the flat piece, not on the wire. Wire tends to heat more quickly than sheet, so watch the heat color and redirect the flame if this happens. Solder flows toward the hottest area, so heat the side of the wire opposite the solder placement. The heat will draw the flowing solder under the wire.

When the solder forms a fluid, shiny seam, remove the flame immediately and pickle.

SOLDERING WIRES TO WIRES

Soldering parallel wires or tubes together is similar to wire-sheet soldering because only a minimum of surface contact is made between the pieces. Make sure that the pieces are clean, properly fluxed, and in contact with each

Solder placement for soldering the drilled unit at right angle to a base piece. A clip of soft iron wire holds the upright piece in position. The torch flame will be applied from the side opposite the solder placement.

Completed right angle soldered joint.

other. Pins may be placed in the charcoal block to hold the wires together.

Very little solder will be needed, but there must be a snippet at each end of the joint. Heat the pieces uniformly until the solder flows, then remove the pins with tweezers (they will be hot). Pickle, then rinse the piece in clean water.

ANGLE SOLDERING

Soldering a standing strip of metal to a flat surface requires some ingenuity. If the strip is curved, it will stand alone, but if it is straight, it must be braced with steel pins or iron binding wire.

Clean and flux the joining areas and place snippets along one side of the joint so that they lie flat on the base and touch the vertical section.

Heat slowly from the side opposite the solder placement. The upright piece will tend to heat more rapidly than the base piece, so try to heat both pieces evenly until the solder flows.

Remove any bracing wire or pins, before pickling the soldered unit.

COMMON SOLDERING PROBLEMS AND THEIR CAUSES

Seam does not fill with solder	This is usually caused by a poor fitting of the parts, inadequate fluxing, or the presence of dirt.
Solder forms into balls and does not flow	This may occur when the solder reaches its melting point before the surrounding metal has reached the same temperature. It can also be caused by an insufficient application of flux.
Soldered joint is porous and pitted.	This is usually caused by overheating or by dirty solder.

SOLDERING COPPER AND BRASS

Copper and brass can be hard soldered with silver solders using the procedures previously described. This type of soldering forms a strong, neat joint that is nearly invisible. Sheeting and wire or both can be satisfactorily soft soldered if equipment for hard soldering is unavailable.

The solid, thin wire form of soft solder, available in coils and spools, is recommended for copper and brass jewelry work. Soft solder requires a special flux, such as the commercial paste No-Ko-Rode.

Procedures for soft soldering:

• Be sure that the joining surfaces fit exactly.

• Clean the surfaces thoroughly according to methods previously described.

• Apply paste flux to the contact areas and position snippets along the joint.

• Heat with a small propane torch, only until the solder flows. Too much heat will boil the flux, oxidize the metal, and prevent the solder from flowing.

• Cool the piece, then scrub it with hot water and detergent to remove the remaining flux. *Do not pickle pieces with soft soldered joints.*

• To join one flat surface to another, flux the underside of the top piece and melt snippets on this surface to form a thin coating. Cool the piece. Reflux the solder surface and place the piece, solder side down, upon the bottom piece. Heat both pieces until the solder melts and joins them. Cool, then clean the piece with hot water and detergent.

• If necessary, the metals may be bound together for soldering with soft iron wire.

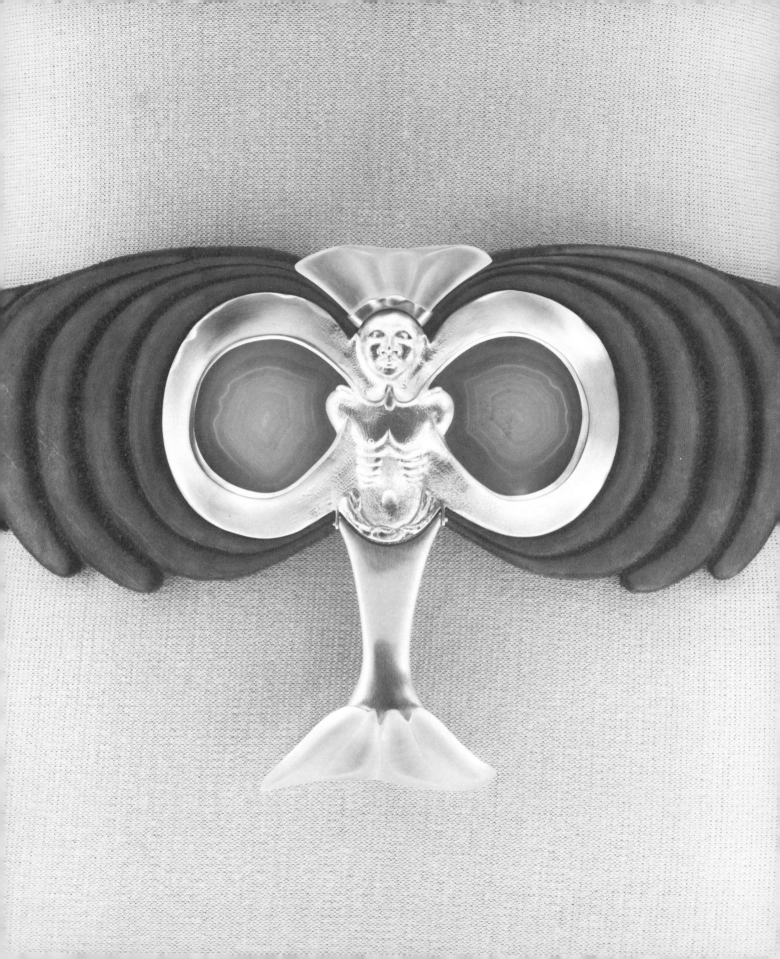

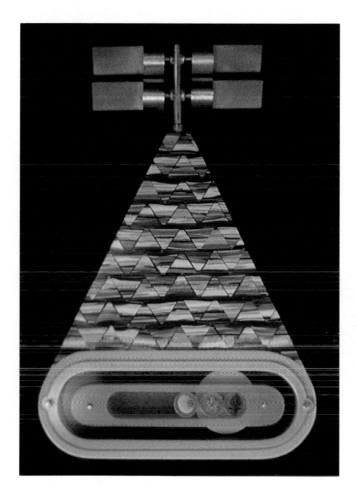

above: Brooch by Bob Natalini. This picture shows the more than forty
different colors of triangular tiles Natalini created by pour-laminating
over polyester.

left: Waist ornament, *Merman* by Marcia Lewis. Sterling silver, agate,
resin and leather; fabricated, cast and repousséd. Buckle, 7″ × 9″ (17.8
cm × 22.9 cm). Lewis feels that *Merman* utilizes a variety of materials
that jewelry students will find interesting.

top: Bracelet by Charles Loloma. Sandcast gold surrounds five lander blue turquoise stones. The inside is inlaid with turquoise, coral, lapis lazuli, and other materials. Photograph by K. J. McCullough. Loloma interprets his design: "The stones on the outside are arranged to emphasize the line of strength of the hand which follows a path from between the index and middle fingers to the inside of the wrist. The hidden inlay is meant to symbolize the inner qualities of the wearer."

bottom: Gladiator Belt by Deborah E. Love Jemmott. Strip-woven copper with a leather interior.

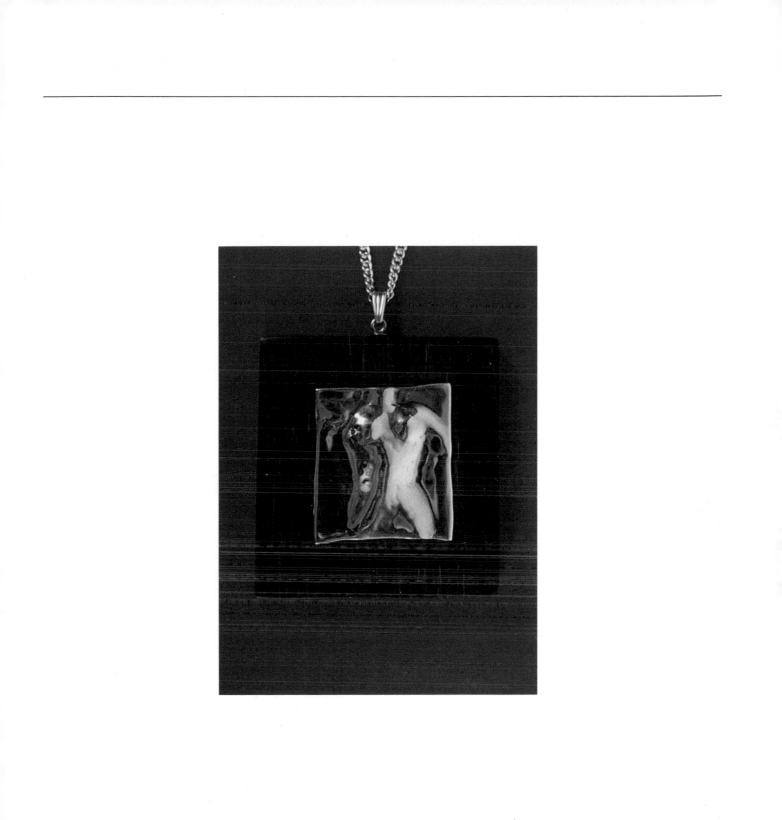

above: Torso by the author. Sterling silver repoussé pegged to
rosewood.

above: Bottom view of the bell by Deborah E. Love Jemmott.

right: Bell by Deborah E. Love Jemmott. This picture shows how the silver and Delrin polyester are accented by the copper and brass.

top: Brooch #6.5 by David W. Keens. Aluminum, brass, Delrin, enamel paints, and epoxy-enamel.

bottom: Hand Pendant by Bob Natalini. This detail captures one of the light patterns programmed into the thirty-five light-emitting diodes imbedded in the beetle's body.

above: Pendant by the author. Sterling silver fused and constructed and pegged to black walnut wood.

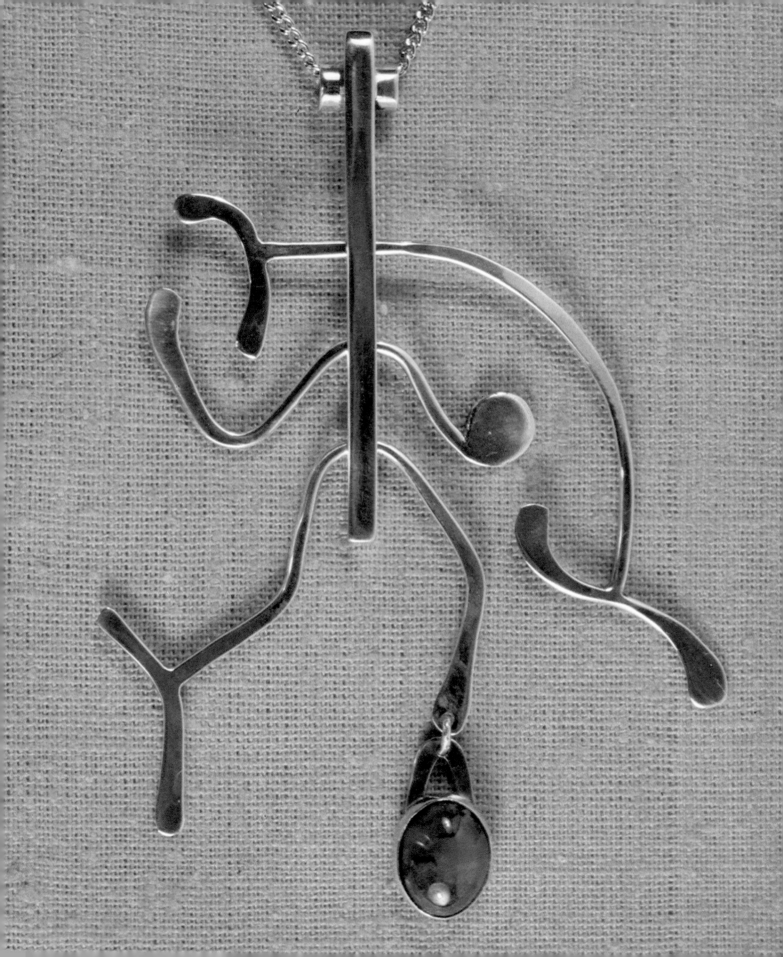

CHAPTER 5

Forging, Forming & Shaping

above: Bracelet by John T. Fix. 4 gauge sterling silver, forged. Photograph by Mark Habicht.

left: Pendant by the author. Sterling silver formed and forged. Curved mobile parts are hinged through the square vertical center. Bezel-mounted moss agate is attached with a jump ring.

Metal's full potential as a decorative material is not often realized until its malleability is exploited to create dimension. Most jewelry metals can be worked — bent, twisted, formed, forged, or shaped — to produce sculptural qualities, from domes to textures, and to establish movement and form as well.

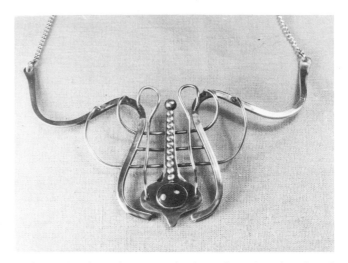

Neckpiece by the author. Lapis lazuli, sterling silver forged, and constructed.

Annealing

The forging and shaping of silver and other jewelry metals is a forcing process. As metal is hammered, bent or twisted, its molecular structure is compressed and tempering (hardening) occurs. It becomes brittle, difficult to shape, and may flake or crack. When metal tempers during fabrication, it must be annealed (softened) with heat from the torch.

Anneal small pieces on the charcoal block and larger pieces in an annealing pan filled with lump pumice. Long lengths of wire should be coiled and temporarily bound with iron wire while being annealed in the pan.

Annealing should be done in a dark area so that the metal's temperature can be determined from its changing color. Silver is effectively annealed at temperatures between 900° to 1200°F (482° to 650°C); its color will range from faint red to dull red. When this temperature is attained, remove the flame and allow the silver to cool until the red color disappears.

Copper and brass anneal at approximately 1000°F (538°C). Their color at this temperature is also faint to dull red.

A long length of wire coiled for annealing in a pan filled with lump pumice.

Forging

Forging is as old as the discovery of metals. Fundamentally, forging hammers metal to force a change in dimension.

A wide variety of hammers, stakes, and anvils is used by silversmiths, but the beginning jewelry maker can forge effectively with a clean, polished bench block, some clean peening, and planishing hammers.

Experiment with forging by hammering scraps of copper sheet and wire on a steel block with a cross peen hammer, a ball peen hammer, the peen end of a chasing hammer, and a planishing hammer. Hammer strokes should be rhythmic with the weight of the hammer being utilized to develop an even force. Notice how different hammers change the metal's dimensions and surface texture; how the metal becomes more resistant to dimensional change as tempering occurs.

Forging wires and strips of silver for jewelry designs can help to create interesting changes in the relationships of width and thickness. Rhythm and movement can be achieved by forging wire into various widths. Hammers can bring metal surfaces to life with textures that reflect and sparkle.

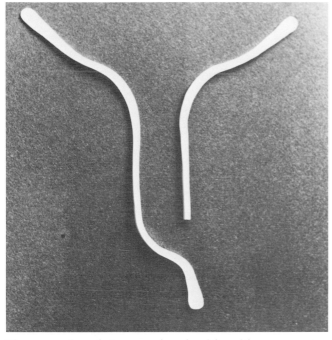

These parts of a neckpiece were shaped and forged from square wire. Notice how the varying width establishes movement and rhythm.

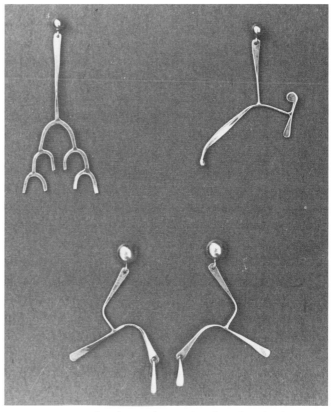

Earrings constructed with round wire, then forged to develop more interesting dimensions in the wire.

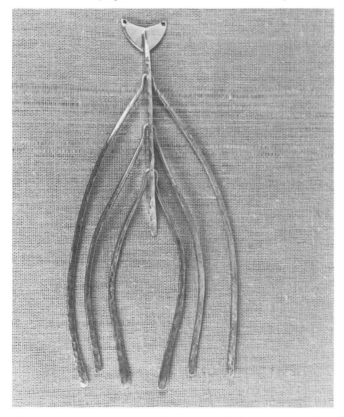

The free-moving units on this pendant were made from round wire that was forged with a ball peen hammer after the wire was in place.

Hair ornament by Clara Schlegel. Sterling silver, forged, linked, and constructed. Photograph by Larry Langdon.

Dapping

Dapping is a method of forming a dome or hemisphere from a metal disc by using a dapping block or die and dapping punches. A dapping die is a polished steel block with various sizes of shaped depressions machined into the surface of the block.

The disc to be domed should fit within the depression on the dapping die. If it overlaps the depression, the outer edges may be marred when the punch is struck. Start with a depression larger than the finished size desired. Punch the disc and then progressively move to the next smaller depression until the desired size is reached. For each successive punching operation, use a punch that is slightly smaller than the depression to compensate for the thickness of the metal being shaped. Dapping causes tempering and necessitates annealing.

Finished domes can be soldered to a background piece or suspended by jump rings. If a dome is soldered to a background piece, its edges must be filed smooth to make a good fitting joint. Also, a small hole should be drilled in the background piece and centered beneath the dome. This allows the gases generated during soldering to escape; otherwise, they would cause gaps in the soldered seam.

Domes and cupped forms can also be raised with a ball peen hammer and a lead block. The lead block method is effective for raising domed areas within a flat piece of metal. Remember to clean away any lead particles before soldering.

Domes can also be formed by using a cutout wooden block for dapping.

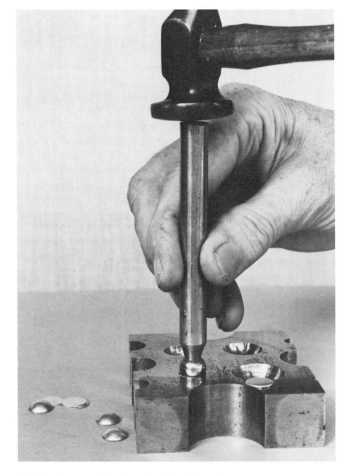

Forming domes with a dapping die and punches.

Forming Wire

Thin wire and large, smooth curves in heavier wire can often be shaped by hand. However, small intricate shapes and shaping heavy wire are better achieved using pliers with contoured tips similar to the contours being formed in the wire. Round nose pliers should be used to shape curved forms. The flat nose or chain nose pliers should be used to make angular bends and corners. Narrow strips of metal can also be shaped with these pliers. Experiment with scrap copper wire and strips to develop a feeling for pliers as forming tools.

The jaws of pliers used for forming should be smooth and polished to avoid marring the surface of the wire. If necessary, pad the jaw faces with masking tape.

Small, unwanted curls, bends, and kinks in wire can be straightened with careful pressure from flat nose parallel jaw pliers. Wire can also be straightened by rolling the kinked area between two blocks of soft wood or by gently hammering it with a rawhide mallet on a block of soft wood. Straighten thin wire by clamping one end in a vise and pulling the other end with a pair of heavy pliers until

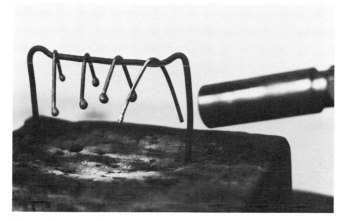

Method for suspending wires for fusing the ends into spheres with the torch. The center wire is just beginning to melt.

The ends of a wire to be twisted are clamped in a bench vise and the other end is looped over the hook in the hand drill. The hook is pulled to keep the wire taut as the drill is turned.

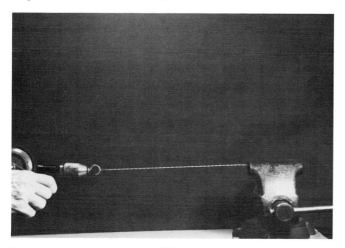

Twist forming in the wire as the drill is turned. Notice that the wire is held straight and taut.

Round wires were end fused, soldered together at their center, then shaped with round nose pliers to create this pendant.

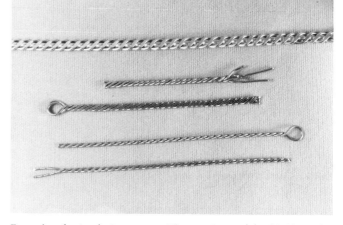

Examples of twisted wire patterns. The top piece and the third from the top were hammered on a bench block.

the wire stretches. Because wire will be hardened by pounding, rolling, or stretching, it should be annealed before it is reshaped.

When the design calls for it, wire twists can be made easily. Simply loop the wire(s) around a hook that is fastened into the chuck of a hand drill and secure the wire ends in a bench vise. Pull away from the vise as the drill is turned. Only annealed wire should be twisted in this way. Additional surface effects can be achieved by hammering the twisted wires on a steel block with a planishing hammer.

Experiment with the method by twisting various combinations of scrap copper or brass wire. Try combining different gauges of wire. Twist two thin wires together, then twist the strand with a pair of heavier gauge wires. Try a single strand of square wire. Hammer some of the twists and notice how the patterns change. Such experimentation will help in choosing the best pattern for your jewelry.

Twisting tempers wire and it should be annealed before it is further shaped.

Curving and Bending Sheet Forms

Sheet metal is curved and bent with a rawhide mallet and such forming devices as bracelet mandrels, ring mandrels, silversmithing stakes, or forms made from pipe or wooden rods. Angles and corners can be formed by pounding the metal over the edge of an appropriately shaped block of wood. Corners formed in this way will always be rounded and somewhat flowing because the metal will not compress enough to make a sharp bend. Sharp corners should be constructed by soldering pieces together.

If the beginning jewelry maker does not have such equipment as silversmithing stakes, there are other methods. Pounding the metal with a round face wooden mallet into a depression carved in a block of wood is one alternative. Pounding it over a rounded form carved from wood is equally effective. A lead block and a ball peen hammer can produce the same result.

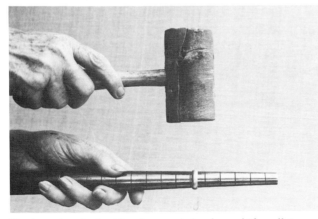

Shaping a ring shank with a ring mandrel and a rawhide mallet.

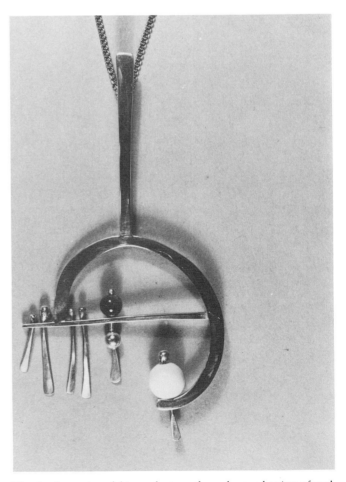

The circular section of this pendant was formed around a piece of steel pipe. The mobile vertical units were flattened after being inserted in the holes.

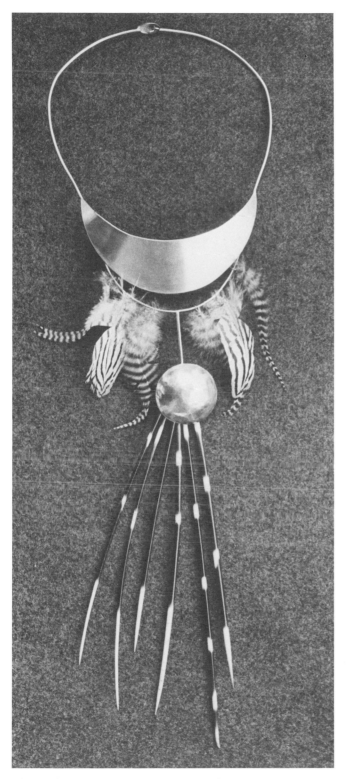

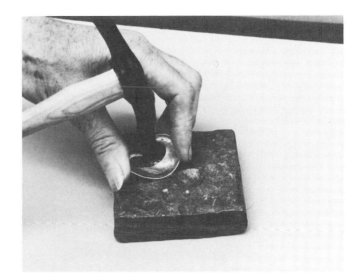

A peening hammer and lead block are used to curve a surface. The block was first molded with a rounded depression.

Repoussé and Chasing

Repoussé is a technique for creating relief in metal and requires considerable practice before it is mastered. The relief is created by using hammers and punches to form a design through the reverse side of a piece of metal. The metal is mounted on a supportive material that compresses as the shaping occurs. Chasing is done on the front side of the piece to further define the form and texture the surface after a design has been brought into repoussé relief. The simplified description of the processes described here will serve as an introduction. For more information, refer to an advanced jewelry text that covers repoussé and chasing in detail.

A piece of 24 or 26 gauge silver larger than the design to be raised is imbedded in chaser's pitch, a compound of pitch, tallow, pumice, and linseed oil that is simultaneously rigid and resilient. The pitch will yield when the metal is struck with chasing tools. Being careful not to ignite the pitch, slowly warm the steel or cast iron bowl of pitch with the torch. Warm the metal also. Handle the warm metal with tweezers and place it on the softened pitch. Push the metal into the softened pitch with the tweezer tips so a little of it oozes up over the edges of the metal. Cool the pitch until it is firm.

A tracer, a thin edged tool with rounded corners, is used to make a thin outline of the design that will show in relief on the opposite side of the silver. The normal

Silver neckpiece by Carol Anspach. Gently flowing planes of sterling silver enhance the textures and forms of the feathers and porcupine quills. Photograph by Ed Sachs.

A silver form imbedded in pitch being raised into dimension with a chasing tool and hammer.

direction for moving the tracer is toward the body. Tilt the tracer slightly away from its traveling direction and tap it lightly with the chasing hammer. It will slide along to create a smooth, recessed line. Outline the entire design in this fashion, then begin raising the outlined area with the appropriately shaped domed tools.

When the silver is too hard to form with the tools, warm it slightly with the torch flame and lift it from the pitch with tweezers. Turpentine and a coarse cloth or steel wool can be used to remove any pitch that sticks to the metal. Anneal and pickle the piece. If additional raising is needed, replace the piece in the pitch and continue working it.

When the desired depth of relief has been reached, remove the pitch from the piece, anneal and pickle, then replace it in the pitch with the raised side upward. Now further define the raised shapes by working the background and adding any needed surface detail to the raised shapes with appropriately shaped chasing tools.

Continue to model the surface with the appropriate tools. Remember to anneal the metal when hardening occurs. Silver can be stretched to a point where it is structurally weak, so try to limit dimensional changes to only those necessary.

Simplified Relief Forming

Effective low relief designs can be chased on a lead block which yields much like soft pitch. Secure the silver in position by tapping nails into the block around the piece. Clean the silver thoroughly after all such contact with lead.

Simple low relief designs can also be chased using a wood block covered with heavy felt. Chase the metal from both sides.

Pendant by author. Sterling silver repoussé, chased, and engraved.

Bracelet by an unknown Chinese silversmith. Cast, chased, and constructed. Late nineteenth or early twentieth century.

CHAPTER 6

Surface Treatments
&
Finishes

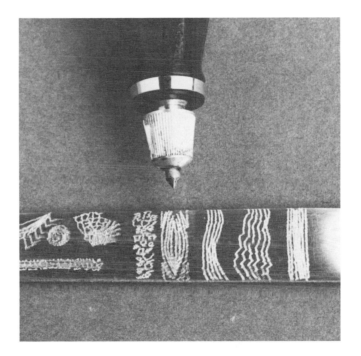

above: textures developed with a vibrating tool.

left: Choker by Clifford H. Herrold. Sterling silver and amber, constructed. Notice the interesting rhythmic texture and line created with twisted wires and the accenting of the forms by oxidation. Photograph by Daniel Grevas.

When surface texturing is called for, it should possess qualities that support the jewelry design, contribute to its unity, and enhance its visual appeal. There is a danger of overdoing surface embellishment; therefore, it should be undertaken with care to assure that it is compatible with and enhances the design. Texture should never be used to cover up poor workmanship.

Texture by Indenting

Texturing by indenting should always be done on the steel block so that the original surface plane is not changed during the texturing process. The following are some of the tools used to texture:

Chasing tools. These are available in assorted end shapes and sizes. Experiment with various combinations of tools and varying hammering force.

Matting tools. These are used to develop background effects in repoussé work and come in many texture patterns and sizes.

Carpenter's nail sets. Various sizes are available to make circular indentations. Try combining marks made from different sizes of nail sets. Tilt the tool for additional pattern effects.

Steel rods and heavy nails. Each of these can be end filed into special shapes and lines and used to texture. These tools will not last long, however, because the steel has not been hardened.

Experiment on scrap copper with the various tools to discover their potential for texturing.

Texture by Cutting

Textures can also be created by cutting, resulting in a sharper edge definition than those produced by pounding or indenting. Some cutting tools used to texture are:

Engraving tools. Linear and crosshatch cuts can be made with a line graver. The piece being engraved must be held firmly enough in a jeweler's vise, or similar device, to free both hands to push and guide the graver. The fine-line graver cuts a number of lines with each stroke. Size 14/8 will produce eight lines at once. In crosshatching, the second cut is made across the original parallel lines, applying somewhat lighter pressure on the graver.

Textures created by different peening hammers.

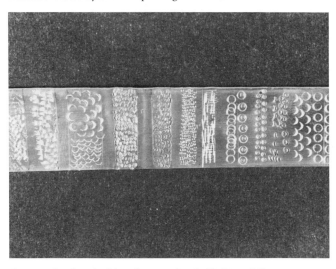

Textures developed with nail sets and nails filed into different points.

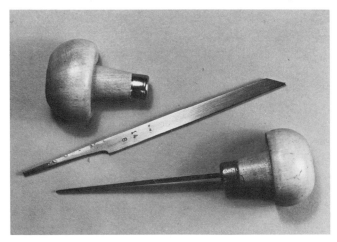

Typical engraving tools used for incising lines.

For a Florentine finish, four series of cuts are required. The first series is made in one direction; the second at a 45° angle to the first. The third series is made at a 45° angle to the second, and the fourth at a 45° angle to the third.

Grinding burrs. Many textures are possible by using grinding burrs powered by a hand tool. Try different burrs and vary the cutting angles to produce different effects.

Vibrating tool. The electric vibrating tool with a reciprocating point can also be used to create texture. Adjust the tool to the desired impact force and try varying the holding angle and point movement patterns.

Pendant by the author. Sterling silver, fused and engraved, set with a black pearl. Background linear texture was engraved with a vibrating tool.

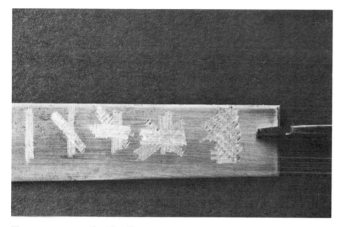

Textures engraved with a line graver.

Texture by Fusing

Fusing is a nonsoldering joining technique used to join small pieces of wire, coarse filings, or granules of silver scrap to a heavier base piece. Interesting granular surfaces can be created by fusing. To texture by fusing, use a base piece of 20 or 22 gauge silver. Pickle, rinse, and dry both granules and base. After all the silver has been fluxed, position the granules and heat until all the metal takes on a shimmering, shiny appearance, but does not flow. Remove the flame, cool for several minutes, pickle, and rinse. Do not heat beyond the shimmering stage or the entire piece will melt.

Fusing is a semicontrollable design process. The arrangement of the granules being fused should be in harmony with the overall design. If they are shifted by bubbling flux during the first stages of heating, reposition them with a scriber, then continue to heat.

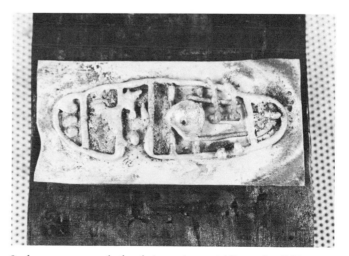

Surface appearance of a fused piece prior to pickling and polishing.

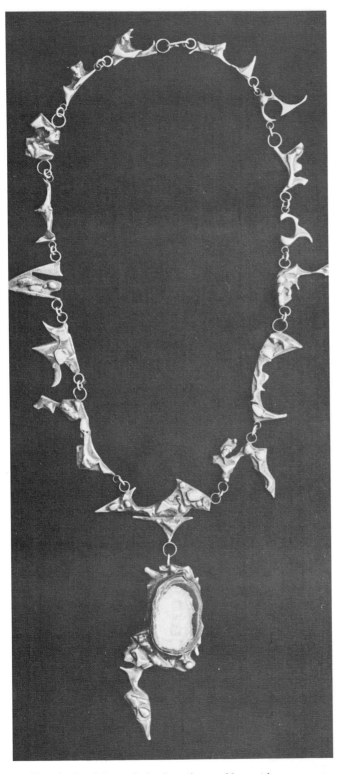

Pendant by the author. Sterling silver, fused and constructed, set with a blue pearl. Granular background effect was produced by fusing coarse filings to the base.

Necklace by Carol Anspach. Sterling silver necklace with rose quartz. The design is composed entirely of constructed and fused units that have been linked together. Photograph by Ed Sachs.

Pendant by the author. Sterling silver, reticulated and constructed, with blue lace agate stone.

Reticulation as a Texture

Reticulation is a heating technique that wrinkles the surface of silver into an entangling pattern of ridges and valleys. Although an alloy of 83 percent silver and 16 percent copper is best suited for the process, sterling silver can also be reticulated if the annealing-brushing preparation is done carefully.

To develop the fine silver outer skin needed for reticulation, heat the piece to its annealing temperature, rinse and brush it with brass wire and soapy water. After this heating-brushing treatment has been repeated four or five times, anneal once more, but this time pickle and rinse only. Do not wire brush. To allow for trimming, the prepared piece should be made larger than required for the design.

The prepared piece now has an inner core of sterling silver and an outer skin of fine, nearly pure silver with a higher melting point. When the piece is heated, the inner core will melt first and cause the fine silver to reticulate.

Place the prepared silver on an asbestos pad and heat it with a full torch flame. Keep the flame moving because too much direct heat will melt the fine silver and create a hole in the piece. Carefully heat until the entire surface wrinkles.

Pickle and rinse the reticulated piece and trim it to suit its intended location in the jewelry. Reticulated silver is brittle and is usually used as a flat section in a design because it may crack if it is bent or formed. Use easy solder to attach the piece to the design.

REMOVING FIRE SCALE

Fire scale is oxidized copper that burns into the surface of silver during soldering or annealing. It is gray or purplish in color and usually not visible until polishing begins. If the scale is not removed, it will tarnish faster that the surrounding metal and appear as a discoloration.

Fire scale can be prevented by fluxing all surfaces exposed to the torch flame during soldering and annealing. However, this method is not always advisable because the bubbling of such a large amount of flux may shift the snippets and the parts being joined. Fire scale formation can be minimized by thorough cleaning and

Napkin Rings by Deborah E. Love Jemmott, 1978. Sterling silver, reticulated and constructed.

Fire scale is visible on this annealed sterling silver panel.

Scotch stone must be used with water to remove scratches. Immersing the scratched area in water while rubbing with the stone works well.

pickling and by avoiding overheating or prolonged slow heating during soldering.

Fire scale may be removed by carefully rubbing the discolored area with fine emery paper (No. 340) until the surface takes on a uniform, soft, satiny appearance. Rub the emery lightly so that deep scratching is not caused.

Stubborn fire scale can be removed by dipping the piece into a room temperature solution made from equal parts of nitric acid and water (remember: to mix acids, the acid is added to the water). First, scrub the piece clean. Then suspend it on a stainless steel wire and dip it into the solution for only two or three seconds. Rinse the piece in water. The fire scale will have turned black and can be removed by rubbing the piece with pumice and water. Repeat the dipping and rubbing operations until no black remains.

Nitric acid is highly corrosive. Use it carefully and provide full ventilation for the work area.

Fire scale can also be covered with fine silver by following the reticulation surface preparation procedure. Care must be exercised in building up the surface because abrasive or prolonged buffing will remove the fine silver skin and again expose the fire scale.

REMOVING SCRATCHES AND FILE MARKS

Before a finished piece of jewelry is polished, all scratches and blemishes should be removed. Remove deep scratches and marks with an appropriately shaped file of the finest cut that will work. Remove file marks with No. 340 emery paper and refine further with No. 400 emery paper. Rub the emery in several different directions so abrasions are not accented. Scratches inaccessible to emery paper can be removed with a scotch stone, which can be shaped with a file to fit the blemished area. The scotch stone must be used with water, preferably under water. If it is used dry, it will cause additional scratching. After smoothing with emery paper or scotch stone, the jewelry should be thoroughly cleaned with soap and water.

To remove blemishes, start with the finest cutting agent that will work. This will save time and tend to preserve the original surface quality.

Finishing and Polishing

In addition to its superb working characteristics, silver lends itself well to finishing. Silver is highly reflective and can be given a mirrorlike shine, a soft satiny luster, or a flat matte surface. The finish chosen should be appropriate for the design, but should also retain its original surface quality.

Brilliant, mirrorlike finishes tend to show wear quickly and are not appropriate for jewelry such as rings and bracelets, which are subject to frequent contact and abrasion. Such contact will not mar a satin or matte finish, however.

Earrings, pendants, and pins will retain a brilliant

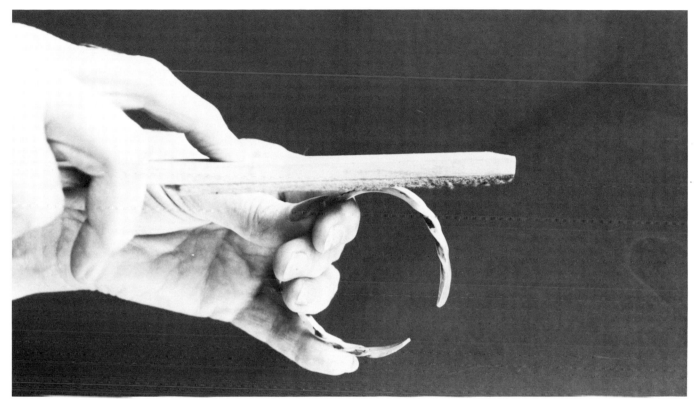

Polishing a bracelet with a hand buffing stick. Polishing compound is applied to the felt pad which is rubbed briskly against the metal.

finish well, but when not being worn, this jewelry should be kept in a tarnish-proof pouch. If tarnishing occurs, it can be removed and the brightness restored with a rouge impregnated cloth

After removing the blemishes and scratches, finish the surface. Grade 4/0 steel wool rubbed in one direction will produce a satin, matte finish. Polishing compounds, applied with a buffing stick or powered buffing unit, can produce a variety of finishes.

To use the buffing stick, coat the felt with the polishing compound and rub it briskly back and forth over the metal, changing directions constantly. Because their cutting actions differ, a different buffing stick should be used for each compound. Scrub the jewelry with detergent and warm water after each buffing operation.

The motorized buffing unit is an indispensable tool for the school art room or the jewelry maker's studio. The motor should be equipped with tapered spindles to permit the easy changing of buffing wheels. It should have a shaft speed of 1750 to 3400 rpm, the higher speed being used for the small polishing wheels. A 5-inch buffing wheel on a 1750 rpm motor will handle most polishing operations.

These are the most commonly used polishing compounds:

Tripoli. This fast cutting abrasive refines the finish left by emery paper and leaves a dull finish on silver.

White diamond. This cutting compound leaves a soft semibright luster on silver.

Green compound. This polishing agent gives a slightly grayish, high luster to silver.

Red rouge. This polishing agent is used to develop a brilliant finish.

The most commonly used polishing wheels are the following:

Felt. Felt buffing wheels are used for controlled polishing and are available in flat edge, knife edge, and tubular for polishing the inside of rings. A felt wheel is best for flat surfaces and edges, but it will groove or wave a surface that is not moved constantly.

Muslin. Both firm and soft muslin wheels can be used with all compounds. Green compound and rouge produce a better polish when used with soft wheels.

Chamois. This leather wheel is used with rouge to develop a brilliant luster.

USING THE POLISHING LATHE

Buffing with powered equipment requires strict observance of safety practices. The wheel turns toward the operator, so the surface being polished MUST BE HELD AGAINST THE WHEEL, BELOW THE CENTER LINE OF THE MOTOR SHAFT, MIDWAY TO THE BOTTOM (between 7 and 8 o'clock — refer to the photograph on buffing). The force is downward and away from the operator when the work is held in the proper location. The piece being polished should be held with both hands, and a face shield or safety glasses should be worn. Keep loose fitting clothing, long hair, and dangling jewelry away from the lathe.

Apply the buffing compound sparingly and by holding the bar or stick against the spinning wheel at the polishing location described in the preceding paragraph. Use a separate wheel for each compound and identify it on the side of the wheel to prevent mix-ups. Remember, the finish is developed by the polishing compound, not by the buffing wheel. Use firm pressure, and resupply the wheel with compound as needed.

Start with tripoli and proceed to the finer compounds until the desired finish is attained. After each polishing operation, thoroughly scrub the jewelry with a washout brush in water and detergent.

Do not buff more than necessary to bring about the desired surface. Both tripoli and white diamond are abrasive enough to remove details and round off corners.

A clogged buffing wheel may be cleaned by holding a coarse file against the rotating wheel to loosen the fibers. Hold the file in the same position used when buffing.

POLISHING HARD TO REACH AREAS

Intricate wire loops, the inner edge of cutouts, and similar difficult to reach sections of jewelry can be buffed and polished with a nylon cord. Tie one end of the cord to a firm object, pull it tight, and rub the cord with buffing compound. Thread the cord into the polishing area and work the piece back and forth over the tautly held cord.

Hard to reach flat areas can be burnished to a bright finish. Apply a little rouge to the burnisher and rub it firmly back and forth to polish the area.

COLORING SILVER

The attractiveness of a piece of jewelry may sometimes be enhanced by darkening the recessed areas to accent the modeling and the placement of forms. Such shading is commonly done with a solution of potassium sulphide (liver of sulphur). If jewelry is to include a stone, the stone should be set after the silver is colored and polished.

Jewelry must be absolutely clean before applying the coloring solution. It should be pickled, scrubbed with detergent and water, rinsed, allowed to dry, and then handled with a facial tissue to prevent finger marks from interfering with the action of the solution.

Prepare the solution by dissolving a bean-sized lump of

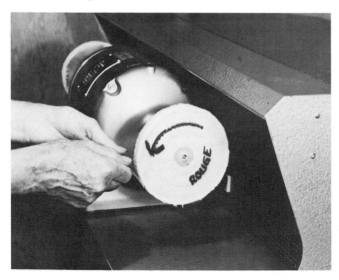

Parts being machine buffed must be held against the polishing wheel below the center line of the motor shaft, midway to the bottom as shown in the illustration. The arrow indicates the direction of wheel rotation. A separate wheel should be used for each polishing compound. Mark the wheels to avoid mixups.

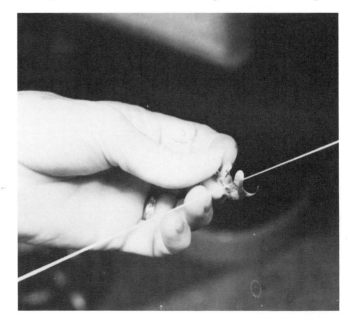

Buffing a hard to reach inside surface with a cord coated with polishing compound.

potassium sulphide in 4 ounces of hot water. Both the dry chemical and the prepared solution deteriorate rapidly when exposed to light and air, so store them in dark amber glass containers with tight lids and mix only small quantities of the solution at one time.

There are two ways to use the solution: either dip the piece into warm solution and and leave it until the desired color is attained, or brush the solution onto selected areas. When it blackens sufficiently, rinse the piece under running water, then allow it to dry. If the solution is left on the metal too long, the colored areas will flake off. If this happens, pickle the piece and start over. Always cover the solution after removing the jewelry.

Potassium sulphide solutions release a pungent odor and should be used with adequate ventilation.

Commercially prepared colorants for silver are available in liquid form from jewelry making suppliers. These solutions are usually made from ammonium sulphide, have very little odor and produce a dense black color. Even though their cost is somewhat higher than potassium sulphide, they may be better suited for classroom use. The surface preparation and procedures are the same as those for potassium sulphide.

After the excess color is removed, the desired highlighting is achieved by rubbing the selected areas with your finger or thumb and wet, fine pumice powder. Rub with a circular motion until the desired luster is attained. Try to blend the bright area into the black area so that the tonal change is gradual. When the desired effect has been achieved, thoroughly rinse the jewelry in running water to remove all the pumice. If additional brilliance is desired, carefully polish the bright areas with a small, soft felt wheel and white diamond compound or rouge.

The pumice and water method of polishing leaves an effective, long-lasting finish on silver and it can be used to prepare the final surface for many jewelry designs.

COLORING COPPER AND BRASS

The following chemicals can be used for coloring copper and brass.

Potassium sulphide. Same procedures as those used for silver. Resulting color is charcoal gray.

Ammonium sulphide. 1 gram to 7 ounces of water. Use as a hot solution and dip the metal. Resulting color is black.

Copper nitrate. 1½ grams to 6 ounces of hot water. Apply hot solution with a brush. Resulting color is sage green.

Copper sulphate. 1 part to 2 parts water. Use as a hot solution and dip the metal. Resulting color is brown.

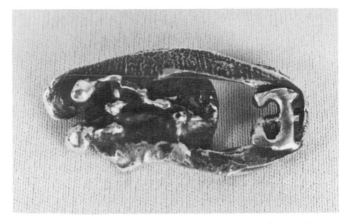

This fused and reticulated pendant was chemically darkened, then the highlights and textures were defined by rubbing it with a pumice and water paste.

CHAPTER 7

Combining Metal with Other Materials

above: *Buffalo Rings and Ivory Ring* by Deborah E. Love Jemmott. Rings were fabricated from sterling silver and inlaid with ivory and buffalo horn.

left: Pendants made from teak (top left); zebrawood (top right); rosewood (bottom left); black walnut (bottom right).

Although metal is the basic jewelry material, many contemporary jewelry makers combine such materials as wood, plastics, bone, and found objects with metal in their designs.

In planning jewelry that combines materials, the designer should strive to create visual appeal and maintain design unity while preserving the wearability of the piece. Research and experimentation may help in assessing the advisability of combining a particular material with metal.

The following section discusses the characteristics and working properties of several materials often used with metal.

Wood

Many hardwoods possess color and grain qualities that can enhance the beauty of jewelry. The color subtleties and line rhythms vary from species to species and from piece to piece to provide the jewelry maker with exciting creative possibilities. In addition to their interesting color and grain, the hardness of the woods recommended below add durability to jewelry.

HARDWOODS FOR JEWELRY MAKING

Common name	Basic color	Relative density
Cocobola	dark brown with orange streaks	very hard
Cherry	medium reddish	hard
Ebony	black	very hard
Padauk	shades of red	medium
Rosewood	East Indies — deep red to purple	hard
	Honduras — pinkish brown	hard
	Brazil — brick red to black	hard
Teak	cocoa brown to dark brown	medium
Black Walnut	medium brown	hard
Zebrawood	tan, brown stripes	hard — brittle

These woods may be ordered from craft supply firms and woodworking materials dealers. Usable scrap wood can often be bought from manufacturers of fine furniture.

SHAPING AND SMOOTHING WOOD

Some of the same tools used with metal are suited for woodworking. However, because of the relatively small amount of surface material to be removed or shaped,

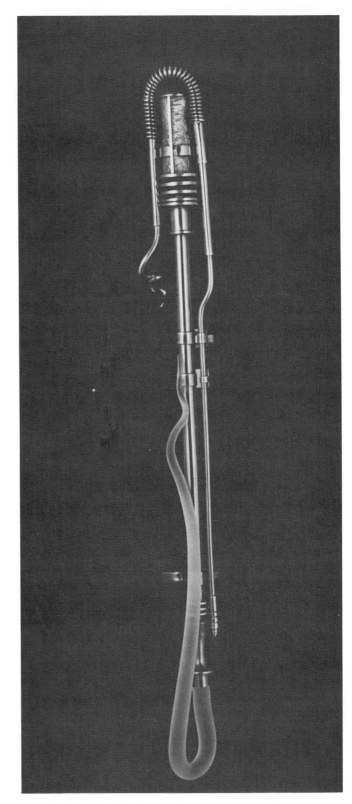

Brooch #3.1 by David W. Keens. Sterling silver and acrylic.

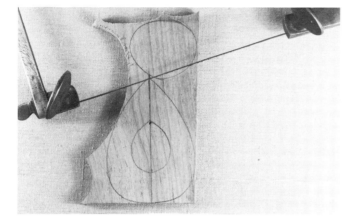

Shapes can be cut from ¼″ (6 mm) thick wood with the jeweler's saw.

Cutting strokes with wood rasps and files should be aligned with the grain.

The surface of rosewood after shaping the ends with a rasp.

most woodworking tools are not suitable for jewelry work. Woodworking tools considered most useful are a sharp knife, a wood rasp, a flat wood file and a half round cabinet file. The new Surform Mini-file (Stanley Tool Company) may be used instead of a rasp. Because the rasp leaves a very rough surface, it should only be used as a quick means of removing thick sections. After the basic shape has been cut with the jeweler's saw, the wood file and the cabinet file will be the tools used most often.

Wood is composed of a variety of cellular fibers that serve the life system of the tree and determine the direction of the grain. The width and types of fibers determine the texture.

Wood is cut and filed more easily when the tool force is in the same direction as the grain. Most wood surfaces cannot be restored after being splintered or chipped by a coarse file or rasp cutting across the grain. When end grain (across the grain) cuts are required, there is a simple way to smooth the end. File inward from the edge and stop slightly beyond the center of the wood. Then repeat, starting from the opposite edge. Do not file completely across the wood.

After shaping the wood with the wood file, sandpaper the surface to a finish appropriate for the jewelry. The first sanding should be done with coarse paper aluminum oxide No. 100 to remove the file marks. Sand with the grain. When all file marks have been removed and the desired form is achieved, continue sanding with a finer paper, such as No. 220 aluminum oxide paper. Finally, sand the surface with No. 400 paper.

FINISHING WOOD

All the woods recommended above should be finished with one of the following preparations to protect the wood and accentuate its grain pattern and color.

Satin finish lacquer, such as Deft, is applied according to the manufacturer's instructions. Three or four coats are usually required. After the final coat has dried, lightly buff the surface to a satin luster with 4/0 steel wool.

Sealer/oil, such as Minwax Antique Oil Finish, is applied according to the manufacturer's instructions.

Toothpicks inserted into the suspension holes of pendants hold the wood while it is finished. These toothpicks are set in a foam block.

Pendant by the author. Cast sterling silver pegged to teak wood. 1¾″ × 2¾″ (4.4 cm × 7 cm).

When the surface becomes tacky, buff it with a soft cloth. Three or four coats are required for a lasting finish.

Beeswax. Soak the wood for one hour in a container of warm, melted beeswax to produce a soft luster on wood. After soaking the wood, allow the wax to cool and set, then buff with a soft, lint free cloth.

Hot linseed oil is applied and buffed in the same manner as beeswax. Wood finished with linseed oil tends to darken with age and it requires an occasional light coat of oil to preserve its luster and to prevent small cracks from developing.

Many other wood finishes are available in addition to those recommended. You may want to practice finishing on wood scraps before choosing the finish which best satisfies the requirements of unity and artistry.

USING WOOD IN JEWELRY

The illustrations in this chapter show wood being used in jewelry in a number of different ways:

In the pendant illustrated, wood is used as a background and support for the metal form. The wood is integral to the design because its shape, color, and grain are all a part of the unity of the design.

To attach the metal design to the wood, first solder a peg of 18 gauge sterling silver to the reverse side of the metal. Then, drill a hole the same size as the peg in the proper location on the wood. Trim the peg so that it protrudes approximately 1 mm (1/32-inch to 1/16-inch) from the back of the wood. Flare (flatten) the wire flush with the back surface by tapping it with the round end of a chasing hammer or a punch. The front of the piece should be padded with several layers of fabric to prevent marring during this riveting operation.

A mounting peg ready for soldering. A loop made from soft iron wire and set into the soldering block holds the peg in position.

Silver strips and wires can be inlaid into lines and holes cut and drilled into wood.

The oval piece of zebrawood will be set in the bezel that is pegged to the walnut panel.

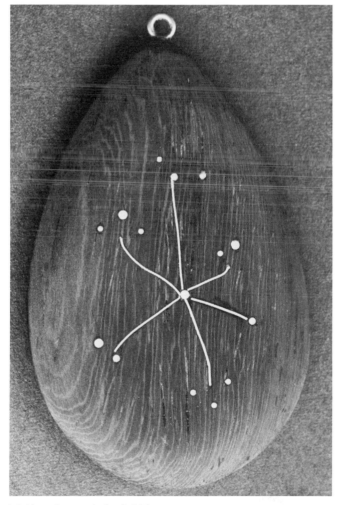

Inlaid pendant ready for finishing.

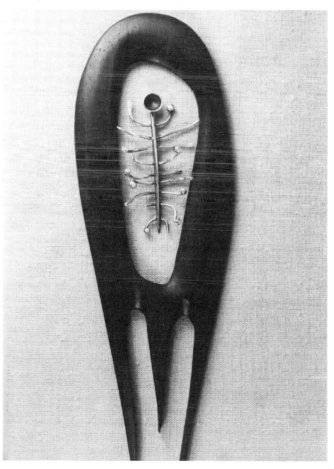

Hair ornament by the author. Sterling silver, constructed and fused with rosewood; 3¼″ × 7½″ (8.3 cm × 19 cm).

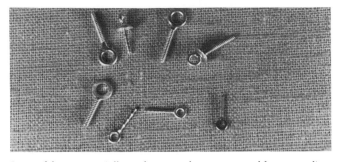

Some of the commercially made pegs and screweyes used for suspending wood and other nonmetallic materials.

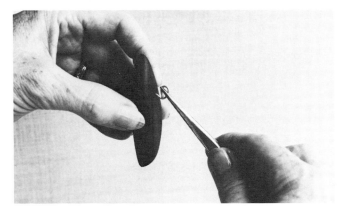

Hook-shaped loop being inserted into a hole drilled at an angle into the wood.

Partially completed pendant utilizing constructed, cast, and forged sterling silver with ebony and dark amethyst.

If the metal attached to the front of the wood is too fragile to withstand the flaring process, the peg end should be glued in place and should not protrude from the back. To prevent the metal from turning, apply contact cement or epoxy between the metal and the wood. Use the epoxy sparingly, so it will not ooze out to damage the wood finish.

Jewelry designs can also be created with wood alone, using metal only for the finding that suspends the piece.

The designer may wish to inlay wood with metal. In this example, fine silver inlay lines the cuts made with a jeweler's saw, and 18 gauge sterling silver wire was set in holes drilled with a No. 60 bit (.040-inch). A starting hole for the saw blade was made with a No. 74 (.0225-inch) drill, which is about the same width as the blade. In developing a design with this technique, avoid patterns that leave short lengths of wood fibers, because the wood will crack and break between the cuts. The metal sheets to be inlaid must be exactly as thin as the narrow saw cuts. Dab a little epoxy glue into the slot, then bend the sheet to conform to the cut lines and tap it into place. After the glue dries, file and sand both wood and metal to a uniform height.

Wood can also be set into metal. A bezel of fine silver was first pegged to the large piece of wood. It will enclose the mounded zebrawood oval. The bezel is pressed against the sides of the mounded oval and bonded to it with cement.

SUSPENSIONS FOR WOOD JEWELRY

Careful consideration must be given to the method of suspending wood-metal pendants. The suspensions should be durable and also well integrated into the unity of the design. Pegs and screw eyes can be bought or constructed from wire and a jump ring or formed from wire with round nose pliers. The finding should fit snugly into a hole drilled at the top of the pendant and secured with a drop of pearl cement or epoxy glue. The point of a straight pin is good for putting glue into the drilled hole.

With large or heavy pendants, a hooked loop may be required. The hole for the finding should be drilled in back at an angle. The weight of the piece is then borne by the wood.

A suspension loop may also be formed by extending a peg on the metal through the wood and then looping it in back with round nose pliers.

Plastics

Jewelry can be made from many plastics, but the polyester casting plastics and the thermoplastic acrylics are best suited for the beginner.

CASTING PLASTICS

Polyester casting plastics are unique because special forms and shapes can be cast or constructed from them and objects can be imbedded within them. Follow the manufacturer's instructions for mold construction, mixing, curing, and finishing.

When a cast polyester form has cured and hardened, it can be shaped, sawed, filed, and drilled with the same tools used for working metal. Saw slowly with a coarse jeweler's saw blade so the plastic will not clog the teeth.

Cast units can be cemented together with a thin film of the casting mixture.

Finishing Cast Plastics

Surface scratches can removed with fine emery paper, then buffed at slow speed with tripoli and an unstitched muslin wheel. Buff lightly and only for short periods. Prolonged buffing causes the plastic to heat up, soften, and absorb the buffing compound. Cool the surface by occasionally dipping the piece in water. Do the final polishing with white rouge and an unstitched buffing wheel. Follow the same procedures described for buffing with tripoli and remember to use a different wheel for each compound. Do not use these wheels on metal after using them on plastics.

PRE-FORMED PLASTICS

Thermoplastic acrylics, such as Plexiglas and Lucite, are available in pre-formed sheets, rods, tubes, and blocks. They can also be shaped, formed, and finished with metal working tools and cemented together with special solvents recommended by each manufacturer. Use the same buffing and polishing procedures for acrylics as for cast plastics.

Many glues, solvents, and plastics are dangerous if inhaled or handled improperly. Always follow the manufacturer's instructions when working with them.

For sources of more detailed information on technical aspects and working procedures for plastics, refer to the Bibliography.

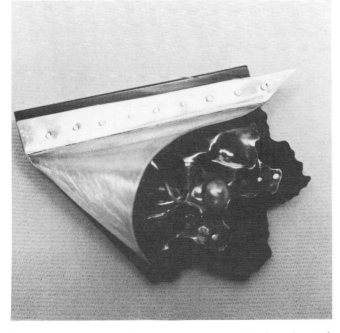

Blue pearl pin by Deborah E. Love Jemmott, 1978. Sterling silver and acrylics with a baroque pearl. Fabricated and riveted.

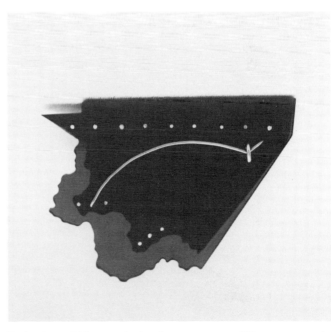

Back view of blue pearl pin. Jemmott states: "The gray area is translucent blue Plexiglas, the white dots are rivets. Backs are important, too!"

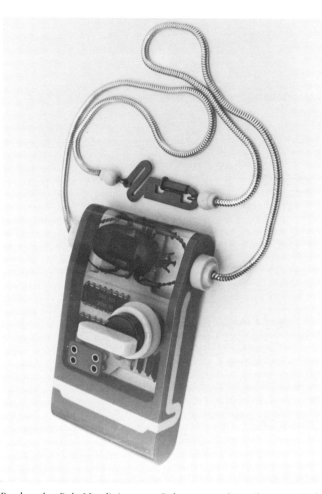

Pendant by Bob Natalini, 1977. Polyester, sterling silver, tropical beetle, and functioning electronics. Embedded beetle has a 35 light (L.E.D.) matrix in its body programmed to flash sequentially. 3½" (8.9 cm) high × 2¼" (5.7 cm) wide.

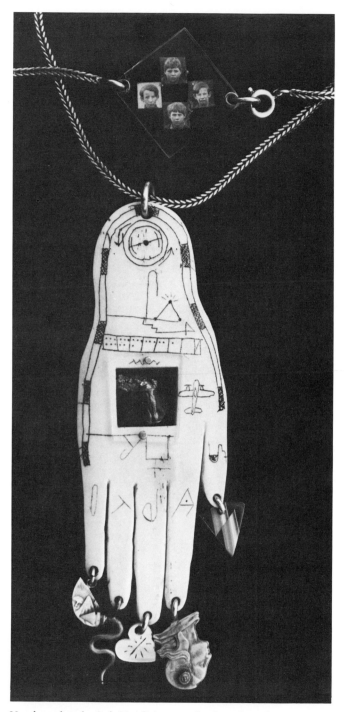

Hand pendant by Bob Natalini, 1976. Sterling silver, bone, copper, brass, ivory, mother-of-pearl, polyester, beetle parts, and photographs. 3½" (8.9 cm) high × 1½" (3.8 cm) wide. Natalini describes this piece: "In this scrimshaw design, some of the elements hanging from the fingers were cut from coins. The beetle parts beneath the Plexiglas-covered windows have different iridescent colors. The polyester-imbedded pictures were cut from a class photograph of the one room schoolhouse vintage."

Bone and Ivory

Bone and ivory can be purchased in slab pieces suitable for use in jewelry. Before being sold, animal bone is thoroughly cleaned and bleached white. Buying pieces that are ready to be worked eliminates the sometimes smelly chore of scraping away the marrow, boiling the bone in alum and soda, and bleaching it with hydrogen peroxide.

Bone and ivory, like wood, are grained and the same precautions for working with wood also apply here, but to a lesser degree. The cutting tools and files used for metal work equally well on bone and ivory, but files used on bone require more frequent cleaning.

Sand each of these substances with No. 400 aluminum oxide paper. Buffed white rouge will provide a final finish. Colored polishing compounds may be absorbed by the grain and should not be used.

Bone and ivory can be carved and shaped to suit a design. Both can be mounted on metal with a bezel mount, prongs, or by pegging with epoxy cement.

Scrimshaw designs can be etched into bone and ivory by first grooving the surface with a sharp scriber or knife. When the grooves are inked with a fine pen point, the resulting eye-catching color contrast and threadlike detail lend a distinctive elegance to jewelry. Use waterproof drawing ink for scrimshaw and sand away any excess ink with No. 400 sandpaper.

Found Objects

Found Objects is a catchall expression for the many objects which, although not usually associated with jewelry, do possess some visual or nostalgic quality that beautifies or sentimentalizes jewelry.

Pebbles, shells, fossils, feathers, insects, and personal memorabilia have been effectively combined with metal by contemporary jewelry makers. Many of these materials are very fragile so it is important that their mountings be sturdy and durable. Fastenings, such as peg mounts, claw mounts, bezels, and cages, are reliable and adaptable for use with nonmetallic materials. Casting plastics and epoxy cements can be utilized for bonding. Some experimentation may help in developing an effective design with the chosen materials.

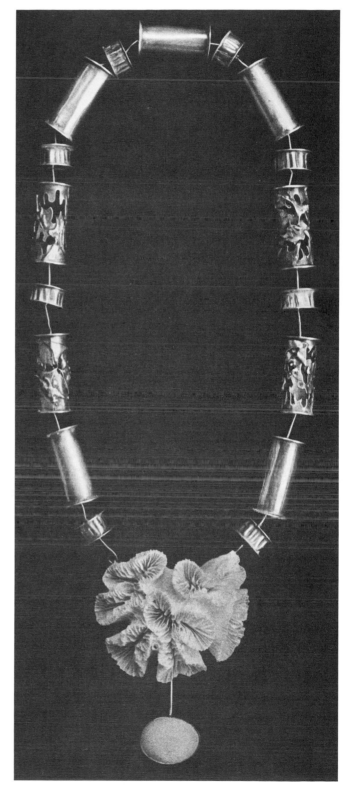

Necklace by Carol Anspach. Sterling silver with coral and a beach pebble. Photograph by Ed Sachs.

CHAPTER 8

Gemstones
&
Settings

above: Face of a ring by the author showing a cabochon black onyx in a typical bezel setting.

left: Some of the more than one hundred gemstones appropriate for jewelry making. The variations in color, shape, form, and texture offer limitless design possibilities.

Gemstones

From earliest times, gems have been valued because of their color and clarity, texture and pattern, their durability, rarity, and sometimes for a mystical power they were believed to possess. Gemstones, like precious metals are commodities whose prices are influenced by supply and demand and by trends in consumer fashions.

Of the more than 2,000 minerals, approximately 100 are cut into gemstones because their visual and physical characteristics make them suitable for use in jewelry. Some organic substances, such as pearls, amber, coral, and shells, are also used in jewelry and are called gem materials.

Gemstones come in a wide range of sizes, cuts, and prices. The selection of a stone, and the design developed to mount it, must be based on the way it contributes to interest and unity. Functional aspects require an equal concern for a gem's hardness, durability, and tenacity.

HARDNESS RATING

The Mohs scale (see Appendix III) is used to rate the surface hardness of ten common minerals, from talc (1) to diamond (10). It rates the mineral's ability to withstand scratching and abrasion, but it is not always a good indication of a stone's resistance to chipping and cracking, which is called *tenacity*. Diamond, for example, has a higher Mohs rating than jade, (7), but it chips more easily than jade. The diamond will chip because of its planes of excellent cleavage (ability to be split). Tourmaline, with a hardness of 7-7½, also has a high resistance to chipping.

Gemstones with a Mohs rating of at least 7 and good tenacity are well suited for rings. Stones with a Mohs rating of less than 7 and stones with good cleavage are better suited for pins, pendants, and earrings, but they can also be used in rings if the design provides a protective setting.

GEMSTONE CUTS

The two basic gemstone cuts are cabochon and facet. The cabochon cut began when our ancestors ground flat or chipped off one hemisphere of their beads. Today, cabochon stones may be round, oval, or free form with flat, low, regular, or high domes. The cabochon cut is used for opaque and most translucent gemstones.

The facet cut is used to shape the surface of transparent gemstones into symmetrical planes (ground and polished) that reflect and refract light.

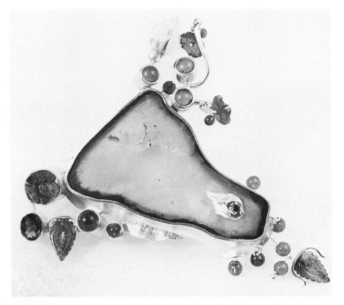

Persian brooch by Marilyn Davidson. Sterling silver, chrysoprase, amethysts, carnelians, amber, citrine, and garnet. 3″ × 3½″ (7.6 cm × 8.9 cm).

Bracelet by John T. Fix. Forged sterling silver. The leaves were made by splitting. The outside element was added. The bezel was also added to hold a small opal triplet. Photograph by Mark Habicht.

Most cabochon gemstones are sized in millimeters. Faceted stones and rare cabochon gemstones are sized and priced by carat weight (1 carat is equal to ¹/₅ of a gram). A carat-size comparison table is included in Appendix II.

PROPERTIES OF COMMON GEMSTONES

The following gemstones are ideal for the beginner's jewelry projects and for classroom use. Good quality cabochon stones in sizes from 8mm × 6mm (¹⁵/₁₆-inch × ¹/₄-inch) to 16mm × 12mm (⁵/₈-inch × ¹/₂-inch) can be purchased for less than one dollar.

Gemstone	Color	Mohs Hardness Rating
Agate		
Banded	Opaque, available in various colors	7
Lace	Opaque, pink or blue, pattern of lacy lines	7
Moss	Opaque with patterning colored mineral inclusions	7
Tree	Opaque with green treelike linear patterns on white	7
Aventurine	Opaque green	7
Bloodstone	Opaque green with red or brown flecks	7
Carnelian	Opaque to translucent red to light brown red	7
Garnet	Transparent deep red	6½-7½
Jasper	Opaque red (also available in more expensive orbicular jasper with striking pattern)	7
Onyx	Opaque black (dyed in bright shades of red, blue, green, and yellow)	7
Quartz		
White	Opaque milky-white	7
Smoky	Transparent light brown	7
Rose	Translucent pink to rose	7
Rock Crystal	Clear	7
Rhodonite	Opaque rose-red, pink, and black	6½
Snowflake Obsidian	Opaque black with white snowflake pattern	5
Tigereye	Opaque brown and brownish yellow (available in various dyed colors)	7

Inexpensive faceted stones are available in smoky quartz, rock crystal, and garnet.

Natural gemstones are also available in polished free form cuts, tumble-polished baroque fragments, polished slabs, natural crystals, and crystal fragments.

SYNTHETIC AND IMITATION GEMSTONES

For a fraction of the price, synthetic gemstones duplicate the color and the physical properties of the natural stones. Fair trade practices and consumer advocacy require that synthetics be represented as such.

A third class of stones, imitation stones, duplicate the color of a gemstone, but none of its physical properties. They are usually made of glass or plastic and because of their fragile nature they are inappropriate for hand-crafted jewelry.

Gemstone dealers are usually quite helpful to those who are selecting stones.

Ring by Clara Schlegel. Sterling silver, constructed with mottled jade. Photograph by Larry Langdon.

Settings

BEZEL SETTING

Cabochon gemstones are usually set in a bezel that is made from a thin collar of silver contoured precisely to match the base of the stone and then pressed in on the stone's sloping sides to hold it firmly. Fine silver is commonly used for the bezel collar because of its higher melting point and greater malleability. However, sterling silver can also be used if it is soldered carefully.

To fashion a collar for a cabochon stone, cut a strip of 26 or 28 gauge silver wide enough to extend from the bottom of the stone up to the beginning of the slope of the stone, usually about ⅛-inch (3 mm). Wrap it around the base and mark it for the exact length needed to enclose the stone. Then, with the jeweler's snips, cut the strip slightly beyond the end mark to allow for filing. File the ends of the strip smooth and be sure that it fits tightly around the stone when the two ends meet. Only a perfect fit will assure and secure bezel.

After the strip is properly fitted to the stone, remove the stone and bring the ends together firmly and precisely. Place the collar on a charcoal soldering block to flux it. Place one or two snippets of medium or hard solder on the outside of the collar so that they overlap the joint. Heat until the solder flows into the joint and then pickle the piece. After rinsing and drying the bezel, use a fine file to remove any excess solder.

The bezel should fit snugly enough to barely touch the stone, allowing it to pass through the loop with a minimum of pressure. If the stone can drop through the bezel, it is too loose and should be cut open at the joint, resized, and resoldered. If the bezel is too small, it can be gently enlarged by placing it on a ring mandrel or smooth metal rod and tapping it lightly with a rawhide mallet.

After the bezel has been shaped to fit the stone, it must be soldered to the piece of jewelry that will contain the stone. Plan this soldering as the final soldering operation

Bezel strip is wrapped tightly around the base of the stone and marked for cutting.

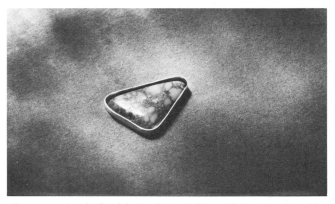

Always examine the fit of the bezel strip before soldering it in place. The bezel should barely touch all sides of the stone.

Enlarged view of a bezel strip positioned on a charcoal block for soldering. Note that the solder pieces bridge the ends to be joined. Grainy substance is residue from a self-pickling flux.

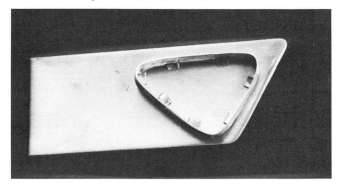

The completed bezel is soldered in place with snippets placed around the inside of the strip so that they touch both base and bezel.

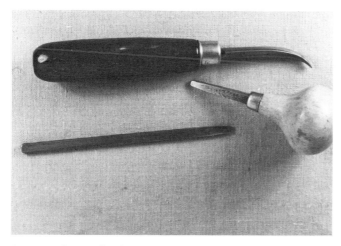

A stone pusher or a flat-faced chasing tool can be used to press the edge of the bezel against a stone. The curved burnisher is used to further tighten and smooth the bezel.

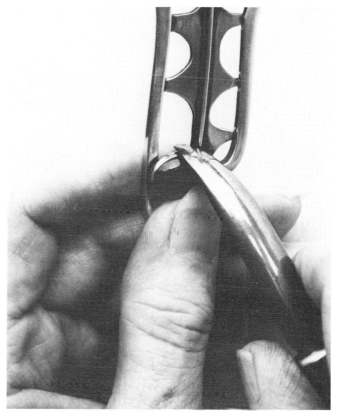

Using a curved burnisher to further tighten and smooth a bezel.

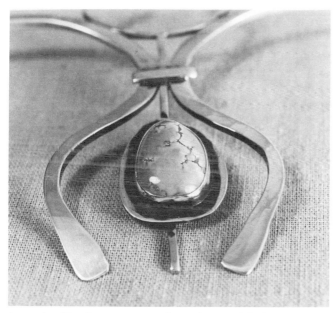

A completed bezel mount in a pendant. The smooth high luster of the bezel edge is a result of rubbing with a curved burnisher.

A shouldered or bearing bezel has a flat strip soldered around the inner circumference to provide a supporting ledge. Be sure enough bezel remains above the ledge to secure the stone.

required in constructing the jewelry. File the bottom edge of the bezel so that it perfectly fits the surface plane on which it is to be soldered without leaving any gaps. Check the fit of the stone after filing to be sure that the bezel was not bent out of shape. Position the bezel, flux, and place easy solder snippets around the inside of the bezel so that they touch both the bezel and its base. Concentrate the torch flame on the base area first. The bezel and the base should reach the melting point of the solder at the same time so that it will flow into the joint. Pickle and rinse. Remove all excess solder from inside the setting.

Compare the height of the bezel to the height of the stone. The bezel should rise just beyond the beginning of the slope of the stone. A high bezel is difficult to fit over a stone since a greater surface area of metal must be compressed. If the bezel is too high, carefully file the top of the bezel until the appropriate level is reached. Remove the file marks with a scotch stone or fine emery paper.

Before setting the stone in the bezel, the jewelry should be polished to completion. Chemical coloring should also be completed before the stone is set because some gemstone materials are affected by the oxidant.

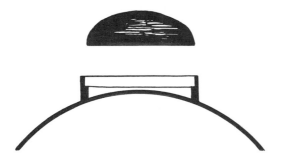

Diagram showing how a bearing bezel is used to mount a flat-based stone on a curved surface. The bottom of the bezel is filed to match the contour of the base.

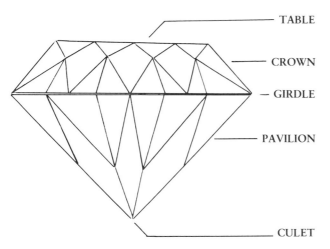

TABLE

CROWN

GIRDLE

PAVILION

CULET

The terms used to identify sections of a faceted stone.

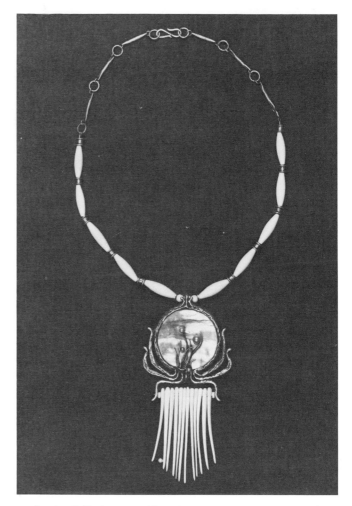

Pendant by Clifford H. Herrold. Sterling silver, abalone, ivory, and blue pearls. Cast and constructed. Photograph by Daniel Grevas.

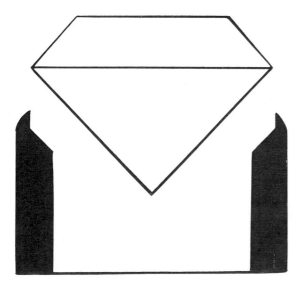

Diagram of a setting for a faceted stone. Each prong is cut or filed to create a shoulder that matches the angle of the stone's pavilion. The metal above the shoulder should be thin enough to be bent against the sloping crown of the stone to firmly hold it in place.

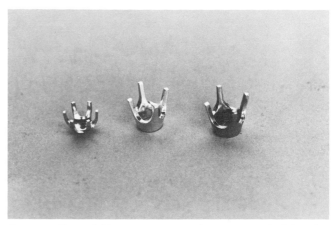

Commercially available prong settings. The setting on the left is for pearls or beads. The prongs of the other two settings must be notched to provide a shoulder for a faceted stone, and to form a prong which must be bent over the crown of the stone.

Setting for a faceted stone constructed from sheet silver. Note the angled shoulder for the pavilion and the thin prongs that will be bent over the crown.

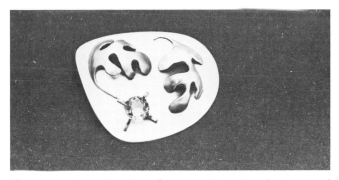

The prong setting with a faceted stone in place. Note the amount of reflected light allowed through the stone by the open prong structure.

Prong setting constructed from square wire and square tubing.

Filing a notch in the square setting to create a shoulder and prong.

Notch with an angled shoulder has been filed on the right prong. Other prongs will be filed exactly the same.

Position the stone in the setting and place the jewelry on a firm, smooth work surface. Small jewelry and pieces that are difficult to hold may be mounted in a ring clamp, engraver's block, or nylon-faced jeweler's vise. While holding the stone flat with one finger, push the top edge of the bezel against the stone with a stone-setting pusher or a flat, square chasing tool. Press a small section of the bezel against the stone and repeat this on the opposite side. Work around the stone by alternately pressing opposing sections until the entire bezel is in place. The bezel will tighten more when it is burnished. Burnish carefully with a firm, smooth rubbing pressure to avoid scratching the metal.

This bezel construction may be adapted to meet the specific needs of a particular design. Transparent cabochon stones can be better illuminated by setting them over a hole cut in the base. When the base of a stone is rounded or irregular or when a stone with a flat base is to be mounted against a curved surface, such as a bracelet, a flat ledge, called a *bearing*, is required within the bezel to hold the stone level and firm. The bearing, made from 18 or 20 gauge silver, is soldered to the inside of the bezel, leaving enough of the bezel above the ledge to secure the stone. A bearing bezel is shown in the illustrations on page 83.

Prong setting developed for a coco geode. Cupped disc has an opening sawed to match the contours of the geode.

Side view of the geode mounting shows how the prongs support the top plate and clamp the geode securely.

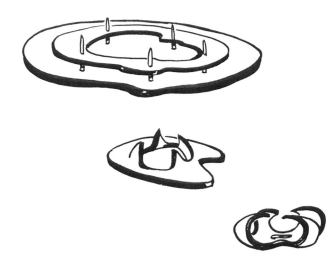

The construction or selection of mountings for crystals, uncut gem materials, and stones with irregular surfaces presents challenges. Some construction possibilities are shown.

PRONG SETTING

Faceted stones are usually mounted in prong settings. This open mounting permits a high degree of light reflection and refraction, which enhances the qualities of the stone. Less formal prong settings are also used to mount irregular uncut stones and crystal fragments.

Prongs can be constructed from square wire, round wire, or flat sheet thick enough to securely hold the stone. The size, shape, and number of prongs needed will actually depend on the stone's size and shape and the desired design, but at least four equally spaced prongs should be soldered to the base.

Notch the inside edge of each prong to provide a shoulder to hold the stone. The bottom of these grooves should be sloped to match the angle of the pavilion (bottom section) of the stone. Be sure each of the prongs is grooved at the same height and that the metal above the groove is long and thin enough to be bent over the crown of the stone. Shape and smooth the prongs with a small file. Polish the constructed form before setting the stone. When the stone is in place and resting evenly on each shoulder, burnish the ends of the prongs tightly against the crown of the stone. Work alternately and gradually from opposing sides until all the prongs fit tightly against the stone. Be sure no sharp edges remain when the prongs are in place.

Many different prong settings are used by jewelry designers. For more advanced instruction concerning the mounting of faceted stones, refer to the Bibliography.

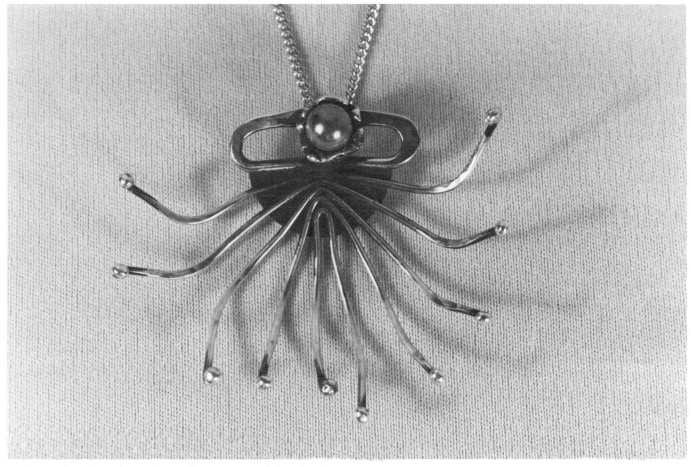

Pendant by the author. Blue pearl pegged in a constructed, forged, and fused sterling silver form.

PEG SETTING

Many gemstones and gem materials, such as pearl, ivory, and coral, can be purchased in the form of half-drilled beads. This type of bead is fastened with a wire peg soldered to the jewelry.

To make such a peg mounting, drill a hole of the same diameter as the peg wire into the jewelry. Cut a peg longer than needed and slide it into the hole in the jewelry. Slide the bead all the way onto the peg, so that the bead contacts the jewelry. Remove the bead when the peg position has been so determined and solder the peg in place. Cut off the peg section that protrudes from the back of the jewelry. Roughen the peg with a file, coat it with epoxy glue or cyanocrylate adhesive, put a drop of glue in the bead hole, and mount the peg. Follow the adhesive manufacturer's directions. Be sure to do the required polishing and finishing before glueing the bead in place.

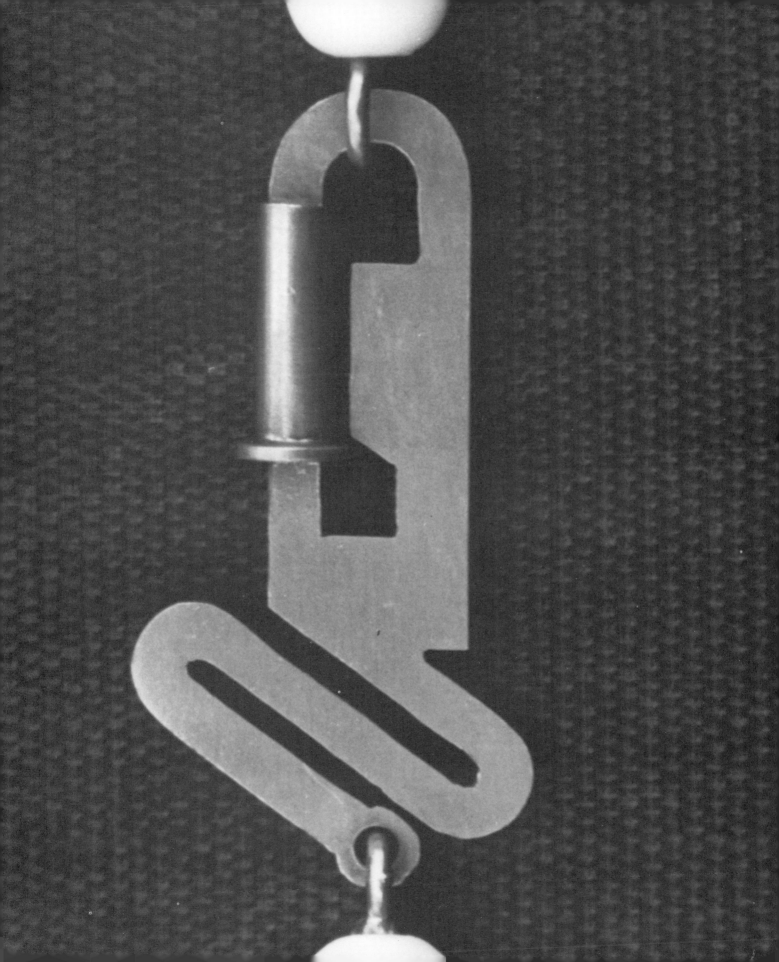

CHAPTER 9

Findings
&
Fastenings

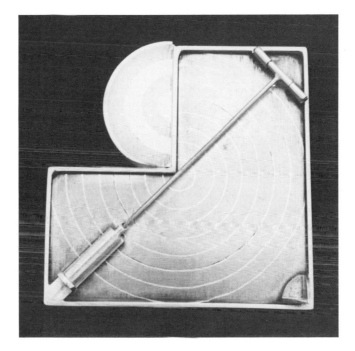

above: Back view of the geometric brooch by Deborah E. Love Jemmott (see illustration in Chapter 2). The pin back clasp on the lower left is spring-loaded. Pulling on the bottom plate releases the pinback. When the plate is released, the spring in the tubing captures the pin tong.

left: Spring-load pendant clasp designed by Bob Natalini for the beetle pendant (see illustration in Chapter 7). Notice how the round forms emphasize the transition from the chain to the clasp. The clasp's resemblance to an electronic printed circuit makes it compatible with the pendant.

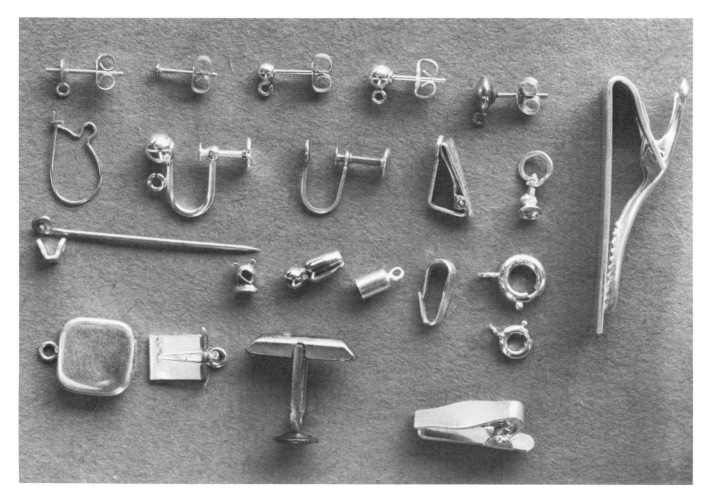

Findings is a generic term used to categorize a wide variety of holding, fastening, mounting, and pinning devices, such as ear wires, ear posts, jump rings, spring rings, catches, clasps, pin backs, cuff backs, bails, and screweyes.

For the beginning jewelry maker who is not yet able to construct delicate and durable parts, the excellent commercial units are a recommended alternative. Many professional jewelry makers use commercial fasteners for pin assemblies, ear wires, ear backs, tacks, and other parts that are not visible when the jewelry is worn. When a finding will be visible, most professional jewelry makers integrate it into the unity of the design.

The selection or construction of findings requires care because both the enduring wearability and the security of the jewelry depend on their reliability. Treasured handcrafted jewelry should not be compromised or jeopardized by a poorly designed or badly constructed finding. For silver jewelry, select quality sterling silver findings that have been *designed for hard soldering*.

Some of the commercial findings available for jewelry making.
Top row. Left to right: ear post with peg for mounted drilled bead; ear post, plain, with soldering pad; ear post with small ball and drop ring; ear post with large ball and drop ring; ear post with bean and drop ring.
Second row. Ear wire; screw-type ear back with ball and drop ring; screw-type ear back with pad; ear clip; pendant swivel with pad.
Third row. Pin back assembly, joint, tong, and catch; stickpin clutch; cord end; locket bail; two sizes of spring rings.
Fourth row. Box clasp; cufflink back; sweater clip.
Far right, vertical, tie bar back with alligator spring clip.

A cutout suspension loop soldered to the back of a pendant is usually a better finding than a drilled hole fitted with a jump ring.

Attaching Findings

The placement of findings for silver jewelry, such as pins, pendants, and earrings, is an important consideration since the finished piece must be securely and properly suspended when worn. When this placement has been determined, clean both the mounting spot and the soldering pad on the finding, apply flux, position the finding, and place a small snippet of fluxed easy solder so that it touches both the base of the finding and the jewelry. Heat slowly so the finding is not shifted by bubbling flux. If the finding shifts, reposition it with a scriber or soldering pick. It is important to apply the flame to the jewelry, not to the finding, so that the solder will flow properly. When the solder flows into the joint, remove the flame immediately, then pickle, rinse, and dry. Cuff backs and other findings with steel springs should not be pickled because the solution will corrode the springs.

Another method of soldering that works especially well for two-piece findings, such as pin-back assemblies, is to first flux and pre-melt a snippet at the desired location on the jewelry for each pin-back finding. Flux the bottom of the finding, position it on the re-hardened solder, and heat the piece again until the solder flows and forms a shiny line around the base of the finding. With a two-piece pin-back, be sure that the catch assembly and the hinge assembly are aligned so the holding pin will fit firmly into the catch.

Ear posts, tie tack backs, and other similar findings can be held perpendicularly for soldering with a piece of iron binding wire coiled to hold the post or pin, and then bent so that its other end is pushed into the soldering block. (See illustration.) Remember to remove the iron wire before pickling.

A spring ring used as a closure on the end of a chain should not be hard soldered or pickled because both the high heat and the pickling solution will ruin the steel spring in the closure. The spring ring is attached to a chain by first opening the loop on the side of the ring. Slip the end link of the chain over the loop and close the loop tightly with pliers.

Ear post is held in soldering position with a support formed from soft iron wire and imbedded in the soldering block. Snippet is placed so that it touches the base of the post and the mounting surface. Heat will be applied from the side opposite the solder.

The snippets will be premelted and the pin tong hinge and the catch assembly sweat soldered in place. The axle in the end of the tong is inserted into the hinge unit, which is then squeezed closed with pliers after the piece has been soldered, cleaned, and polished.

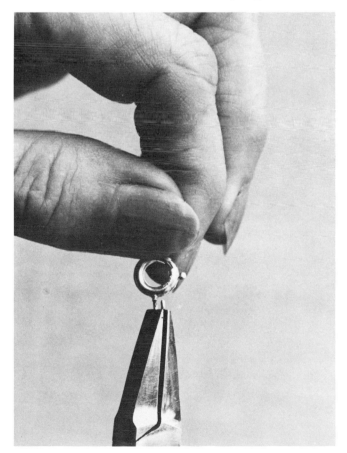

The chain loop on a spring ring is opened and closed laterally with the pliers.

Jump Rings

The common linking device in jewelry making and the basic unit in chain construction is the jump ring. Ordinarily, jump rings are made from round wire; however, square or half-round wire can also be used. The gauge of wire used to construct the ring should be appropriate for the size and function of the ring. Small rings are difficult to form with heavy gauge wire; large rings will not retain their shape if they are made from thin wire.

MAKING JUMP RINGS

Jump rings are easy to make with a mandrel that has a uniform diameter. Simply clamp one end of the mandrel in a vise and wrap annealed sterling silver wire around it in tight, successive loops. After ten or twelve loops are coiled on the mandrel, snip the end wire and slide the coil off the mandrel. The coil should resemble a compressed spring. Thread the jeweler's saw blade through the coil and reset the blade. Fasten the coil in a smooth-jawed vise and saw down through the bottom of the coil. The burred edges on the outside of the rings that result from the saw cut are easily removed with a needle file. The ring ends will join perfectly because of the uniform cutting action of the saw blade.

   The rings now can be closed by pressing the ends together with a smooth-jawed vise or with smooth-faced pliers. To join the ring, spread the ends laterally (so the ring begins to resemble a spiral) and connect them. After the ring is joined, close the ends. This lateral opening and closing will not distort the ring's circular shape or disturb the fit of the joint.

SOLDERING JUMP RINGS

Jump rings that are used to join design units or that are linked together to create a chain must be soldered at their joint. Before soldering, position the joint so that it does not touch any part of the jewelry. It may be necesssary to secure the link by pinning it to the charcoal soldering block or by holding it with a soft wire peg. Flux the ends of the ring and bridge them with a very small snippet. Heat carefully so the solder is not dislodged.

   If rings are being linked together, the joints of links that have already been soldered must be protected from the heat of subsequent solderings. Yellow ochre and water mixed to a pastelike consistency and applied on the soldered joint will provide adequate protection. Remove the yellow ochre with water before pickling.

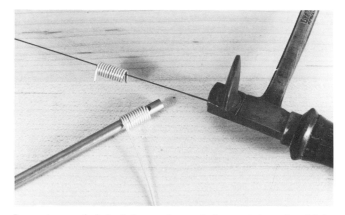

Jump rings and chain links can be made by wrapping wire tightly around a mandrel and then cutting the coil with the jeweler's saw.

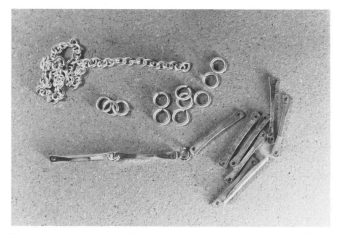

Chains can be constructed in many ways. These are constructed from rings and forged lengths of square wire linked together with jump rings.

A method for holding chain links for soldering. The support is made from soft iron wire and is inserted into a charcoal soldering block.

Chains and Cords

CONSTRUCTING AND POLISHING CHAIN

Commercially made silver chain comes in many styles, sizes, surface finishes, and textures. It can be purchased by the foot or as a complete unit with a jump ring and a spring ring attached. If manufactured chain is chosen for suspending a pendant, select a link style and finish that complement the jewelry.

Many professional jewelry makers design and construct their own chains and suspension systems in order to achieve a completely integrated piece of jewelry.

When this creative approach is chosen, the task of creating a harmonious suspension system depends entirely on the designer's inventiveness and skills. Often, experimentation will lead to a solution. Experiment with link forms by shaping scrap wire with chain nose pliers. Try twisting or flattening the links. Combine different size links. Insert straight items, beads of clay, wood, or gemstones between links. When experimentation leads to a suspension that is harmonious with the design, construct it with silver.

The unity of a pendant chain or neckpiece is even more complete if the end clasp is also integrated into the design and construction. The constructed chain fastenings illustrated can be adapted to suit almost any design and can be constructed rather easily from wire or sheet.

Jewelry with chain or linked suspensions must be polished carefully if a powered polishing unit is used. It is possible for the chain to catch on the buffing wheel and whip around dangerously. Hand polishing with felt and polishing compound is recommended for chain, but if a machine is used, the chain should be wrapped around a rounded piece of wood. The ends of the chain should be securely taped to the board and the board should be grasped so that your fingers press on the taped chain ends. Buff the chain lightly and hold the board so that the chain is buffed lengthwise. Do not buff across the chain.

ATTACHING CORD

Some pendants are more effectively suspended with jewelry cord or a leather thong. Braided nylon cord in ⅛-inch (3 mm) and ³⁄₁₆-inch (5 mm) diameters comes in a variety of colors. Leather can be cut into thongs of any width or purchased in ready-cut square or round thong strips. Once the length has been cut, attach a tubular silver finding, called a *cord end*, to each tip with epoxy cement. After the epoxy has set, fasten a spring ring into one cord end and a jump ring into the other to complete the unit.

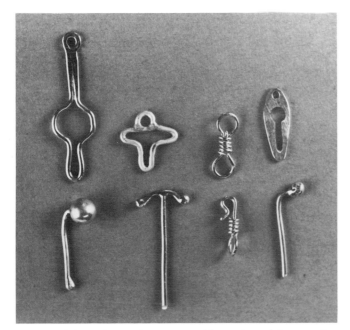

Sample end clasps that can be constructed from wire and sheet metal.

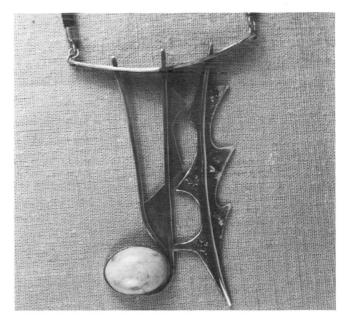

Pendant by the author. Sterling silver, constructed and fused with a rhodochrosite stone. Suspended on a braided, black nylon cord.

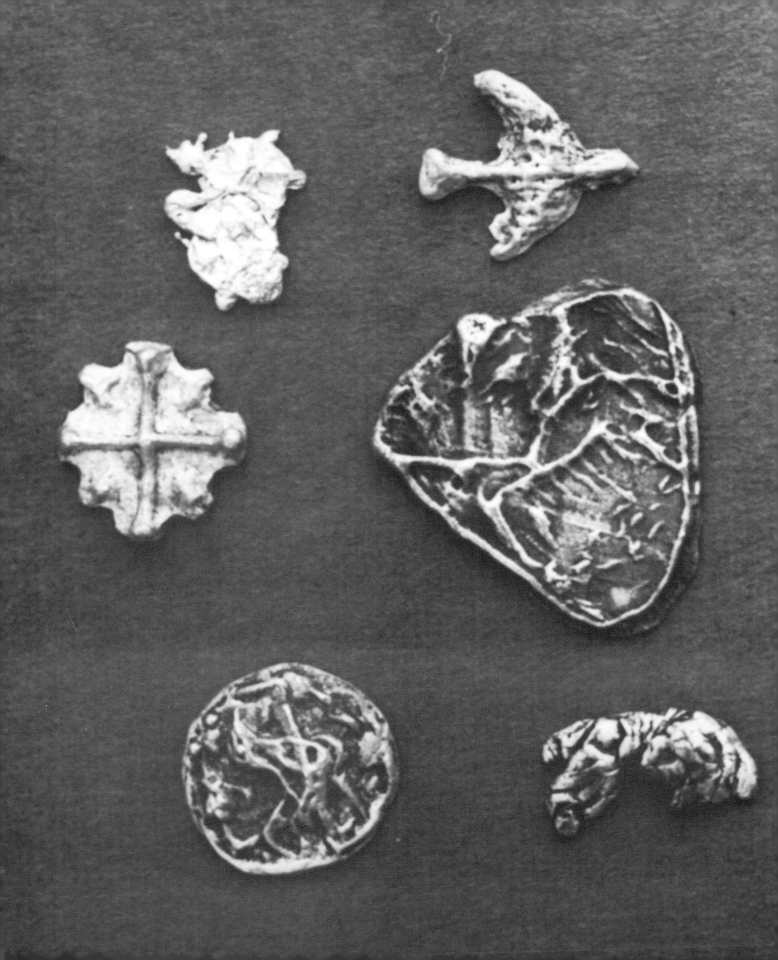

Simple Casting Techniques

above: Pendant by the author. Sterling silver charcoal casting pegged to padauk wood.

left: Charcoal castings.

Metal casting dates back to ancient times and is still an important technique. Lost wax castings are common today among jewelry makers. Yet, lost wax castings were made by Greek and Chinese artisans over two thousand years ago. Contemporary jewelry casting methods are a refinement of this ancient concept. Casting tehniques are also employed by dentists to construct dental inlays and bridging. Lost wax casting is a method of making molds with special forming waxes. By encasing a wax model in a plasterlike material called *investment,* a hollow form of

the model is created when the wax is burned out of the plaster. When molten metal is forced into the hollow, a metal duplicate of the wax model is formed.

Casting molten metal holds a fascination for most beginning jewelry makers. The two simplified casting techniques described in this chapter are ideal for beginners. They require a minimum of equipment and they can provide valuable experience in introducing casting as a forming process. Other casting methods are described in detail in books listed in the Bibliography.

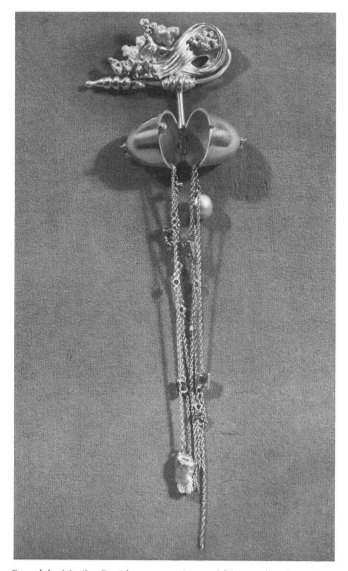

Brooch by Marilyn Davidson, 1978. Cast and fabricated sterling silver with 14K gold, rubies, peridots, garnets, pearls, and tourmalines, 7″ × 2½″ (17.8 cm × 6.4 cm). The brooch detaches from the egg-shaped pendant and can be worn separately. The pendant can also be worn separately on a chain, remaining open as shown, or as a closed brooch with chain and stones tucked inside.

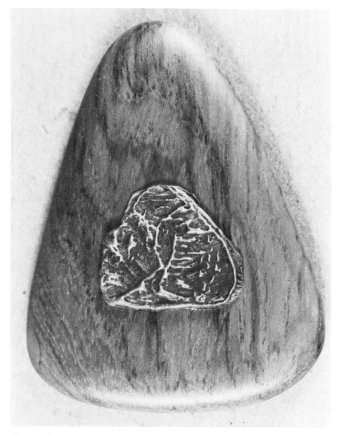

Charcoal cast sterling silver mounted on teak wood.

A cavity for a charcoal casting carved with a fine-pointed stencil knife and a scriber.

Casting in Charcoal

Impression casting with charcoal soldering blocks is a relatively simple process in which one block is the mold and another is used to press molten silver into it.

The first step in charcoal casting is to pencil the design on the surface of a smooth, flat, charcoal block. For a first effort, the design should measure no more than 1-inch (2.5 cm) across. When the design has been drawn, carve it into the block with a scriber, stencil knife, or similar cutting tool. Carve deep enough to give the casting rigidity and remember that the deeply carved sections will become the high areas on the finished casting.

The pressing surface of the second charcoal block should be flat and smooth. The block should be at least 1⅜-inches (3.5 cm) thick and have a surface area of 2¼-inch × 3¼-inch (5.7 cm × 8.2 cm). Its thickness is important because it must be grasped along the edges to prevent dangerous burns from molten silver that can squirt out when the blocks are pressed together.

Place the carved block on an asbestos pad and erect a splash guard around it with strips of sheet metal or wood. These strips should rise an inch or two above the surface of the block to prevent injuries and damage to the workbench.

Estimate the amount of silver needed and fill the carving with scrap wire and sheet that has been pickled and rinsed. Melt the metal until it forms a shimmering ball that rests in the center of the carving. Quickly, evenly, and firmly, press the ball of molten metal into the carving with the other charcoal block. Do not tilt the pressing block or the silver may be squeezed away from the design. Hold the blocks together for several minutes until the metal solidifies.

When the metal no longer shows heat color, carefully invert the mold and drop the casting onto an asbestos pad. If it does not drop, loosen it with pointed tweezers. Transfer this hot casting to the pickling solution with copper tongs. After pickling, rinse the casting and saw off any overextended edges. Then file these edges smooth.

Charcoal molds may be used two or three times if castings are loosened carefully. Charcoal casting is a good way to make pendants, earrings, tie tacks, cuff links, and buttons. It is also an efficient method for making the individual components of a larger design and for making textured background panels for mounting gemstones.

Pieces of clean silver scrap are placed in the mold cavity and fluxed in preparation for melting.

The silver is heated until it becomes molten and forms a shimmering ball. Then, the molten silver is quickly and firmly pressed into the cavity with another charcoal block.

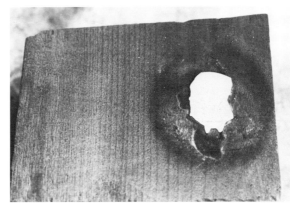

After the molten silver has been pressed into the mold, it should be allowed to cool until all heat color disappers.

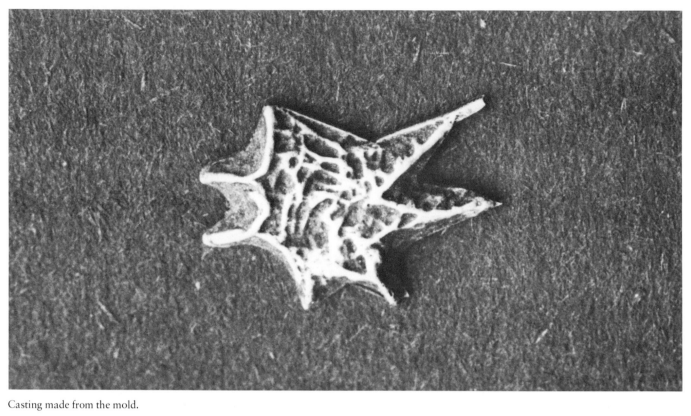

Casting made from the mold.

Charcoal castings were sweat soldered to create these earrings.

Casting in Cuttlebone

Cuttlebone is the internal shell of the cuttlefish and is often used as a mold for small castings. The bone's soft interior can be either carved or impressed to make it into a mold.

To prepare a cuttlebone mold, cut a seven- or eight-inch piece in half lengthwise, using the jeweler's saw. Place a sheet of fine sandpaper on the workbench and sand the soft inside of each half until it is flat and smooth. Place the smooth surfaces together and cut one end so that they are flush. Then saw the other end and both sides to create two matching rectangular pieces.

PATTERN CASTING

To impress the cuttlebone with a harder pattern — wood, plastic, or hardened clay, for example — be sure the pattern has no undercuts. Undercuts are overhanging ledges in the side wall profile of the mold, which will break off when the mold is pulled apart. Place the casting pattern on the soft side of a piece of cuttlebone, with the thickest section of the pattern toward the lower end of the bone and the thinner section about 1½-inches (4 cm) from the top. Press the pattern halfway into the cuttlebone. Place the soft side of the other piece of cuttlebone over the imbedded pattern and slowly press until the two flat surfaces meet. With the pattern in place within the joined halves of cuttlebone, file a groove across each side of the mold to provide a means of later aligning the two cuttlebones.

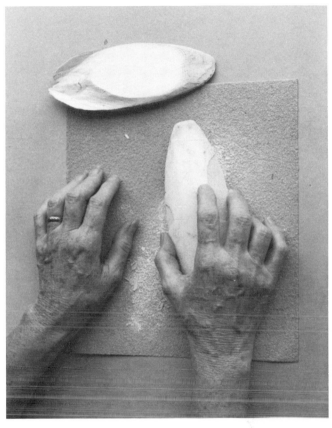

The soft interior of cuttlebone is flattened and smoothed by rubbing it on sandpaper.

Cuttlebone after smoothing and trimming.

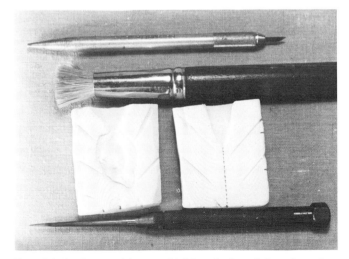

Carved design in a cuttlebone mold. Note the funnel-shaped pouring gate and the vent lines.

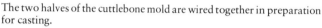

The two halves of the cuttlebone mold are wired together in preparation for casting.

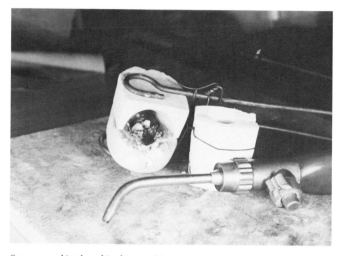

Scrap metal is placed in the crucible. The crucible tongs have been wired tightly together to prevent the crucible from slipping.

Molten silver should be poured smoothly and swiftly into the mold. The torch flame is kept on the metal as it pours.

Separate the cuttlebones, remove the pattern, and examine the impressions to be sure that they are complete. Cut a funnel-shaped opening with a kinfe from the center of the top end of each cuttlebone down to the mold cavity. This opening is called a *gate*, and through it the molten metal will flow down to the pattern cavity. The displaced air and gases that form when molten metal flows into a mold escape through vents that must be scribed into the mold. These vents should be about as wide as a pencil lead and extend from the top section of the mold cavity diagonally upward to the edge of the cuttlebone.

Using iron wire, bind the two cuttlebones together with the grooves aligned. Stand the mold firmly on an asbestos pad with the gate up.

Estimate the amount of silver needed to form the casting, then pickle and rinse the pieces to be melted. Place the metal in a melting crucible. Hold the crucible firmly with crucible tongs and direct the torch flame onto the metal. When the metal shows heat color, sprinkle a little borax into the crucible. Continue heating until the metal forms a shimmering, molten mass that spins under the flame. With the flame remaining on the metal, pour the molten metal swiftly and smoothy into the mold.

When the metal has cooled in the mold, cut the binding wire and remove the casting. With the jeweler's saw, cut away the metal that filled the vents and pouring gate. The casting is now ready for smoothing and finishing.

CARVED MOLD CASTING

A mold cavity can also be carved into cuttlebone with a fine-blade knife and a scriber. Interesting castings can be developed by brushing the carved cavity with a small stiff stencil brush which exposes the texture in the layered structure of the cuttlebone. Experiment with carving and brushing to discover the range of possibilities with this technique.

Follow the casting preparation and pouring procedures described for pattern casting after carving the cuttlebone mold.

right: A cuttlebone casting made by brushing the carved depression with a stencil brush. The texture of the bone's layered structure created an interesting surface.

Measurement of Weight

TROY WEIGHT

Troy weight, which was probably developed at the medieval crafts fairs in Troyes, France, to measure precious metals and stones, is the standard system of weight measurement used in the jewelry trades. The would-be jewelry maker should become familiar with this system of measurement.

The basic measuring units are grains, pennyweight (dwt.), and ounces.

Troy Unit	Metric Equivalent	Avoirdupois Equivalent
24 grains = 1 pennyweight (dwt.)	1.5552 grams	.055 ounces
20 dwt. = 1 ounce troy weight	31.1035 grams	1.1 ounces
12 oz. = 1 pound troy weight	373.24 grams	13.166 ounces

CARAT WEIGHT

Many gem stones are sold by carat weight (not to be confused with Karat [K], which is used to designate the degree of fineness of gold.) 1 carat = $3\frac{1}{16}$ grains troy or $\frac{1}{5}$ gram (200.00 milligrams) metric or .035 ounces avoirdupois.

The carat is further divided into 100 units called points for more exact measurement:

1 carat = 100 points	$\frac{1}{4}$ carat = 25 points
$\frac{1}{2}$ carat = 50 points	$\frac{1}{10}$ carat = 10 points

$\frac{1}{20}$ carat = 5 points

To indicate the weight of fractions of carats, the points are expressed decimally. Thus, a 5.35 carat stone is 5 carats and 35 points.

The size of inexpensive cabochon stones are most often expressed in millimeters. The size of more valuable stones, however, may be expressed in millimeter size and carat weight.

APPENDIX II

Measurement and Weight Equivalents

For the Common Gauges of Sterling
Silver Sheet and Wire

Brown & Sharpe (B & S) Gauge Number	Decimal Equiv. in inches	Metric Equiv. in mm	Sheet Silver Troy Ounce Weight Per Square Inch	Round Silver Wire* Troy Ounce Weight per linear foot
2	.2576	6.54	1.41	3.41
4	.2043	5.19	1.12	2.14
6	.1620	4.11	.884	1.36
8	.1285	3.26	.701	.848
10	.1019	2.59	.556	.534
12	.0808	2.05	.441	.335
14	.0641	1.63	.350	.211
16	.0508	1.29	.277	.132
18	.0403	1.02	.220	.0835
20	.0320	.81	.174	.0525
22	.0253	.64	.138	.033
24	.0201	.51	.110	.0208
26	.0159	.40	.087	.0131
28	.0126	.32	.069	.00821

Note: 1 troy ounce = 1.1 ounce Avoirdupois weight
                     31.1035 grams metric weight

*The approximate weight for square wire per foot can be calculated by multiplying the weight of the same gauge of round wire by 1.27324.

APPENDIX III

MOHS SCALE OF HARDNESS

1 Talc	6 Orthoclase
2 Gypsum	7 Quartz
3 Calcite	8 Topaz
4 Flourite	9 Corundum
5 Apatite	10 Diamond

HARDNESS SCALE RANKING FOR SOME
GEMSTONES AND GEM MATERIALS

2-2½	Amber
2-4	Chrysocolla
3-4	Coral, Pearl
3½-4	Malachite
4-5	Variscite
4-6	Azurite
5	Apatite, Obsidian
5½-6	Lapis lazuli, Sodalite
6	Amanonite, Opal, Moonstone, Tanzanite, Turquoise
6½	Olivine
6-7	Labradorite, Peridot
6½-7	Jade, Zircon
6½-7½	Garnet
7	Agate, Amethyst, Aventurine, Bloodstone, Carnelian, Chrysoprase, Citrine, Jasper, Onyx, Quartz (all varieties), Tigereye
7-7½	Andalusite, Tourmaline
7½	Aquamarine, Morganite
8	Emerald, Spinel, Topaz
9	Ruby, Sapphire
10	Diamond

Note: For comparative reference, a knife blade and window glass have a hardness rank of 5½ on the Mohs scale.

APPENDIX IV

Decimal Equivalent in Inch Measurement for Drill Sizes 1/8" and Smaller

Drill Size	Decimal Equiv.	Drill Size	Decimal Equiv.	Drill Size	Decimal Equiv.
1/8"	.125	47	.0785	65	.035
31	.120	5/64"	.0781	66	.033
32	.116	48	.076	1/32"	.0312
33	.113	49	.073	67	.032
34	.111	50	.070	68	.031
35	.110	51	.067	69	.029
7/64"	.1093	52	.0635	70	.028
36	.1065	1/16"	.0625	71	.026
37	.104	53	.0595	72	.025
38	.1015	54	.055	73	.024
39	.0995	55	.052	74	.0225
40	.098	3/64"	.0468	75	.021
41	.096	56	.0465	76	.020
3/32"	.0937	57	.043	77	.018
42	.0935	58	.042	1/64"	.0156
43	.089	59	.041	78	.016
44	.086	60	.040	79	.0145
45	.082	61	.039	80	.0135
46	.081	64	.039		

APPENDIX V

METRIC LINEAR MEASUREMENT

The basic unit in the metric system of linear measurement is the meter, which is divided into units of 1/10 of a meter (decimeters — dm), units of 1/100 of a meter (centimeters — cm), and units of 1/1000 of a meter (millimeters — mm).

1 meter = 10 dm = 100 cm = 1000 mm

1 dm = 10 cm = 100 mm

1 cm = 10 mm

1 inch = 2.54 cm or 25.4 mm

1 foot = 0.305 m or 30.48 cm or 304.8 mm

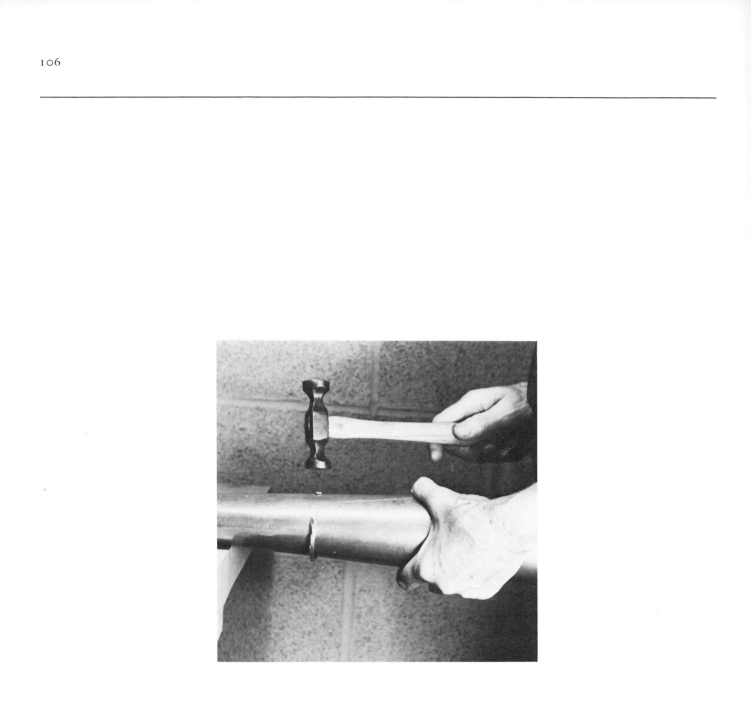

Flattening and forming the ends of a bracelet with a planishing hammer
and a bracelet mandrel.

Reading Resources

JEWELRY MAKING

Chamberlain, Marcia, *Metal Jewelry Techniques*. New York: Watson-Guptill Publications, 1976.

Coyne, John, Edit., *The Penland School of Crafts Book of Jewelry Making*. New York: Rutledge Books, 1975.

Franke, Lois E., *Handwrought Jewelry*. Bloomington, Ill.: McKnight and McKnight, 1962.

Hollander, Harry B., *Plastics for Jewelry*. New York: Watson-Guptill Publications, 1974.

von Neumann, Robert, *The Design and Creation of Jewelry*. Philadelphia, Penna.: Chilton Book Company, 1972.

Winebrenner, D. Kenneth, *Jewelry Making as an Art Experience*. Scranton, Penna.: International Textbook Co., 1955.

JEWELRY MAKING — CASTING

Choate, Sharr, *Creative Casting*. New York: Crown Publishers, 1966.

Kain, Jay D., *Casting Pewter Jewelry*. Worcester, Mass.. Davis Publications, 1975.

JEWELRY-HISTORY

Barsali, Isa Belli, *L'Oreficeria Medioevale*. Milan: Fratelli Fabri Editori, 1966. (English edition translated by Crosland, Margaret, *Medieval Goldsmiths Work*, London: Hamlyn Publishing Group, Ltd., 1969.)

Curran, Mona, *A Treasury of Jewels and Gems*. New York: Emerson Books, Inc., 1962.

Edwards, I. E. S., *The Treasures of Tutankhamun*, New York: Penguin Books, 1976.

Rogers, Francis and Beard, Alice, *5000 Years of Gems and Jewelry*. New York: J. B. Lippincott Co., 1947.

GEMSTONES

Arem, Joel, *Gems and Jewelry*. New York: Ridge Press, 1975. (Available in a paperback edition from Bantam Press, N.Y.)

Dinwiddie, Donal and MacFall, Russell P., *The Complete Book of Rocks, Minerals, Gems, Fossils*. New York: Popular Mechanics Books, 1978.

Sinkankas, John, *Van Nostrand's Standard Catalog of Gems*. Princeton, N.J.: D. Van Nostrand Co. Inc., 1968.

DESIGN

Ballinger, Louise Bowen and Vroman, Thomas F., *Design Sources and Resources*. New York: Reinhold Publishing Corp., 1965.

Brommer, Gerald F. and Horn, George F., *Art: Your Visual Environment*. Worcester, Mass.: Davis Publications, 1977.

Gatto, Joseph A., Selleck, Jack and Porter, Albert W., *Exploring Visual Design*. Worcester, Mass.: Davis Publications, 1978.

Guyler, Vivian Varney, *Design In Nature*. Worcester, Mass.: Davis Publications, 1970.

Malcolm, Dorothea C., *Design: Elements and Principles*. Worcester, Mass.: Davis Publications, 1972.

PERIODICALS

American Craft Bimonthly publication of the American Craft Council, 22 West 55th Street, New York, New York 10019.

Metalsmith Quarterly publication of the Society of North American Goldsmiths. For subscription and membership information: Society of North American Goldsmiths, 8589 Wonderland, N.W., Clinton, Ohio 44216

Rock and Gem Published monthly by Behn-Miller Publishers, Inc., 17337 Ventura Blvd., Encino, California 91316.

Suppliers

The following firms market the listed supplies nationally to schools and jewelry makers.

Local supply sources often appear in the classified section of the telephone directory.

Allcraft Tool and Supply Company, Inc.
  Mail order address: 100 Frank Road, Hicksville, New York 11801
  Sales room addresses: 22 West 48th Street, New York, New York 10036
  204 North Harbor Blvd., Fullerton, California 92632
  Precious metals, tools, equipment, supplies, findings, gemstones, nonferrous metals.
  Catalog: free to schools; $2.50 to individuals (refundable).
  Minimum order: $5.00

Anchor Tool and Supply Company, Inc.
  Mail Order Address: P.O. Box 265 Chatham, New Jersey 07928
  Sales Room Address: 231 Main Street Chatham, New Jersey 07928
  Precious metals, tools, equipment, supplies, findings, gemstones, rare woods, nonferrous metals.
  Catalog: free to schools; $2.00 to individuals.

ARE, Inc.
Mail order address: Box 8, Route 16, Greensboro Bend, Vermont 05842

  Sales room address: Same
  Precious metals, tools, equipment, supplies, findings, gemstones, beads, nonferrous metals, display supplies.
  Catalog: free

Ernest W. Beissinger
  Mail order address: P.O. Box 6165, 24 Red Oak Road, Hilton Head, South Carolina 29928
  Gemstones.
  Sales to quantity users and schools only.

California Crafts Supply
  Address: 1096 North Main St., Orange, California 92667
  Precious metals, tools, supplies, equipment, findings, gemstones.

Castex Casting Crafts
  Mail order address: P.O. Box 1954
  Sales room address: 334 East Avenue 1, Lancaster, California 93534
  Precious metals, tools, equipment, lost wax casting kits, gemstones, supplies.
  Brochure: free

Chaselle Arts and Crafts Co., Inc.
  Mail order address: 9645 Gerwig Lane, Columbia, Maryland 21046
  Sales room address: Same
  Precious metals, tools, equipment, supplies, findings, nonferrous metals.
  Catalog: free
  Minimum order: $15.00

Paul H. Gesswein and Company, Inc.
  Address: 255 Hancock Avenue, Bridgeport, Connecticut 06605
  Branch offices: 676 W. Wilson Avenue, Glendale, California 91203
  76 McCullock Avenue, Roxdale, Ontario Canada M9W 4M6
  Tools, equipment, supplies.
  Catalog: free to schools; $1.00 to individuals.
  Minimum order: $10.00

Greiger's Inc.
  Mail order address: Postal Bin 41, Pasadena, California 91109
  Sales room address: 900 S. Arroya Parkway, Pasadena, California 91109
  Precious metals, tools, equipment, supplies, findings, gemstones, beads, jewelry display supplies.
  Catalog: free
  Minimum order: $5.00

T. B. Hagstoz and Son, Inc.
  Mail order address: 709 Sansom Street, Philadelphia, Pennsylvania 19106
  Sales room address: Same
  Precious metals, tools, equipment, supplies, findings, nonferrous metals.
  Catalog: free

C. R. Hill Company
  Mail order address: 2734 West Eleven Mile Road, Berkley, Michigan 48072

Sales room address: Same
Precious metals, tools, equipment, supplies, findings, gemstones, beads, rare woods, nonferrous metals.
Catalog: free to schools; $2.00 to individuals.
Minimum order: $10.00

Kerr Sybron Corp.
Mail order address: P.O. Box 455
Sales room address: 28200 Wick Rd., Romulus, Michigan 48174
Precious metals, tools, equipment, findings, gemstones, supplies, nonferrous metals.
Catalog: $1.00

Maisel's Arts and Crafts
Mail order address: 1500 Lomas N.W., Albuquerque, New Mexico 87103
Sales room address: Same
Precious metals, tools, equipment, supplies, findings, gemstones, beads, nonferrous metals, jewelry display supplies.
Catalog: free
Minimum order: $25.00

Maxon Co., Unit of GFC
Address: P.O. Box 243, 750 Washington Avenue, Carlstadt, New Jersey 07072
Manufacturer, importer, distributor of tools, equipment, and supplies marketed through a network of dealers in the United States and Canada.
Catalog: free to schools. Orders should be placed with a local or regional dealer.

J. M. Ney Company
Mail order address: P.O. Drawer C-S
Sales Room Address: 13553 Calimesa Blvd., Yucaipa, California 92399
Brochure: free

C. W. Somers and Company, Inc.
Mail order address: 387 Washington Street, Boston, Massachusetts 02108
Sales room address: Same
Precious metals, tools, equipment, supplies, findings, gemstones.
Catalog: free to schools; 50¢ to individuals.
Minimum order: $5.00

Sternwest
Mail order address: 6819 E. Gage Ave., City of Commerce, California 90040
Sales room address: Same
Precious metals, findings.
Catalog: free
Minimum order: $250 silver; $100 gold.

Swest, Inc.
Mail order address: 10803 Composite Drive, Dallas, Texas 75220
Sales room address: Same
Branch offices: 431 Isom Road, San Antonio, Texas 78216
1725 Victory Blvd., Glendale, California 91201
Precious metals, tools, equipment, supplies, findings, gemstones, jewelry display supplies.
Catalog: free to schools; $5.00 to individuals (refundable).

Myron Toback, Inc.
Mail order address: 23 West 47th Street, New York, New York 10036
Sales room address: Same
Precious metals, findings, beads.
Catalog: free to schools; $2.00 to individuals.

TSI, Inc.
Address: 101 Nickerson St., Seattle, Washington 98109
Precious metals, tools, equipment, findings, gemstones, supplies, nonferrous metals.
Brochure: free

Glossary

Abrasive
A cutting substance used with a polishing or rubbing action to produce a variety of surface qualities on metal.

Abstraction
A design or composition based upon a personal interpretation of an object rather than upon exact visual representation.

Amulet
A charm worn on the body and believed to possess protective powers.

Annealing
The process of heating metal to reduce its hardness and brittleness so that it can be more easily formed and shaped.

Baroque
Irregular and curving.

Bezel
A thin metal flange constructed to secure a gemstone.

Brittle
Easily broken or cracked due to hardness and lack of flexibility.

Buff
To smooth by polishing with a cloth or powered wheel. Also, a felt, muslin, or chamois wheel used for polishing.

Burnish
To make shiny by rubbing with a polished steel tool.

Carat
The unit of weight for gemstones. One carat equals $1/5$ gram or $3\,1/16$ grains troy weight.

Chaser's pitch
A mixture of pitch, tallow, pumice, and linseed oil used in chasing.

Chasing
A process for surfacing metal by indenting or embossing it with different tools.

Cleavage
A gemstone's ability to be split along planes.

Compress
A process for making a material more compact by pressure.

Component
One of the parts of a whole unit.

Concave
Hollow and curved like the inside half of a hollow ball.

Conceptualize
To form an idea for a design to be translated into materials.

Convex
Curving outward, as the outside surface of a ball.

Crimp
To bend into shape or pinch together.

Croquis (Krō ké)
A simple, rough sketch.

Cross hatch
Two sets of parallel lines that cross each other.

Crucible
A receptacle, usually made from fire clay, for melting metal.

Dapping
The process of forming metal into domelike shapes.

Embellishment
Ornamentation.

Fabrication
Construction by assembling various parts.

Facet
Any of the polished, flat surfaces cut on a gemstone.

Fibula
A buckle or clasp for fastening garments (ancient Greece and Rome).

Findings
The units used for fastening, hinging, and joining jewelry.

Fine silver
Pure silver.

Fire scale
A gray to purplish oxide that forms on sterling silver.

Flame cone
The shape of the burning gas from a torch or burner.

Fluency
The quality of flowing or occurring smoothly and easily.

Forge
To form or shape metal with blows from a hammer.

Fuse
To join by melting.

Gate
Passageway in a mold for molten metal.

Gauge
A standard measure or scale used to designate the thickness of wire and sheet metal.

Granular
Containing grains or having a grainy texture.

Highlight
A surface made more light reflective and brighter.

Holloware
Serving dishes and tableware made from metal.

Karat
Designation unit for the fineness of gold, $1/24$ part (14 karat gold is 14 parts gold, 10 parts alloy).

Lapidary
One who cuts, polishes or engraves gemstones.

Liver of sulphur
Potassium sulphide.

Luster
The gloss or sheen of a surface.

Malleability
A quality in metal that permits bending and shaping without breaking.

Mandrel
Rods or shapes used as a core around which metal can be formed, shaped, and forged.

Matte finish
A nonreflective, velvety surface on metal.

Matting
The production of a low reflective surface on metal.

Molten
Liquefied by heat.

Nonobjective design
A construction or art form that does not represent any object in nature.

Organic
Having the characteristics of, or derived from, living organisms.

Oxidation
A chemical reaction on metal that changes the surface color.

Pectoral
An ornamental breast plate.

Peen
The ball or wedge shaped end of a forming hammer.

Pickle
A chemical bath to clean metal.

Pickling
To treat with a pickle solution.

Pierced design
A cutout or drilled opening in a design surface.

Planish
To flatten, harden, or smooth metal by hammering.

Porous
Full of small openings or pores.

Pumice
A volcanic rock used in powder form for polishing.

Pyrex
Trade name for heat-resistant glass.

Rawhide
Untanned or only partially tanned cattle hide.

Reciprocating
Moving back and forth.

Repoussé
A process for raising metal from the reverse side to produce a relief design.

Resilient
Springing back into shape or position after being stretched or compressed.

Reticulated
Having a netlike system of veins and ridges.

Rouge
A ferric oxide powder used in stick form to polish metal.

Scarab
A black, winged beetle held sacred by the Egyptians, cut from gem material, engraved, and used as a charm.

Shank
The circular part of a ring that bands the finger.

Snippet
A small cut piece of solder.

Sprue
The opening in a mold through which molten metal flows.

Stake
Wood or metal forms over which metal is hammered to achieve a particular shape.

Sterling silver
Designation for an alloy of 92.5 percent pure silver.

Stylization
Depiction in terms of a style rather than in exact visual representation.

Surface pitting
Small pinpoint depressions that scar metal surfaces.

Sweat solder
Uniting metal by coating one of the pieces to be joined with a layer of melted solder, then placing the pieces together and reheating so that the solder fuses the joint.

Synthesizing
Forming or bringing together separate ideas to produce a single solution.

Tarnish
Discoloration of a metal surface due to oxidation.

Taut
Tightly stretched.

Temper
The hardening that occurs in metals when they are formed and forged.

Tenacity
Toughness, holding together strongly.

Texture
The treatment of a surface to affect a particular appearance or feel.

Translucent
Allowing partial transmission of light.

Transparent
Allowing nearly complete transmission of light.

Tripoli
A light colored, fine siliceous earth used for coarse polishing.

Undercut
An overhanging or concave ledge in the sidewall profile of a mold pattern.

Unity
The integration of component parts to create completeness.

Wood rasp
A coarse file used on wood.

Yellow ochre
A variety of limonite, consisting of iron oxide and clay. Powdered yellow ochre is mixed with water to form a paste that is used as a heat shield for soldered joints.